THE PUBLIC LIBRARY

THE PUBLIC LIBRARY
CIRCUMSTANCES AND PROSPECTS

*Proceedings of the Thirty-ninth Conference
of the Graduate Library School,
April 10–11, 1978*

Edited by W. BOYD RAYWARD

THE UNIVERSITY OF CHICAGO PRESS
CHICAGO and LONDON

THE UNIVERSITY OF CHICAGO STUDIES IN LIBRARY SCIENCE

The papers in this volume were published originally in the LIBRARY QUARTERLY,
October 1978

THE UNIVERSITY OF CHICAGO PRESS, CHICAGO 60637
THE UNIVERSITY OF CHICAGO PRESS, LTD., LONDON

Library of Congress Cataloging in Publication Data
Main entry under title:

The Public library.

(University of Chicago studies in library science)
"The papers in this volume were published originally
in the Library Quarterly, October 1978."
Includes bibliographical references.
1. Public libraries—Congresses. I. Rayward, W.
Boyd, 1939-   II. Chicago. University. Graduate
School. III. Series: Chicago. University. University
of Chicago studies in library science.
Z672.5.P84   027.4   78-19604
ISBN 0-226-70585-4

CONTENTS

INTRODUCTION: THE PUBLIC LIBRARY—A PERSPECTIVE AND SOME QUESTIONS

W. Boyd Rayward

In these introductory remarks, I want to do two things. The first is to suggest a perspective, necessarily personal, for the papers which follow. I want to place our discussion in a context that is historical but perhaps also tendentious. The second thing I want to do is to discuss briefly some of the difficulties we faced in deciding on an approach to partitioning the subject matter of the conference itself. I hope that it will be possible to discern a general theoretical or conceptual coherence in the general subjects of the papers. Though in matters of orientation and detail the authors of these may not agree with each other or with me, and you may disagree with us all, I hope that we can achieve some consensus as to the nature and importance of the questions to which we should give our attention.

The Public Library and Change

In the introduction to the conference program, I observed that "the American public library is one of a number of key agencies in our society. It contains a freely accessible collection of a wide range of educational, informational, and recreational materials, selection among which is almost entirely at the discretion of individual users, whatever their purposes and whatever their age, ethnic, religious, and socioeconomic backgrounds. The public library also provides important services based on its collected materials for widely varying user groups."

1

To this one should add that the public library acts within and for a specific primary community and is supported by that community, which is usually a legally defined and incorporated entity with prescribed authorities and powers. Our emphasis in this conference is integrative. It is on the public library as a community-based agency, whether it is the central library in a great metropolis, or a storefront branch in an inner-city neighborhood, or a town or village or suburban or rural library. At the most fundamental level these libraries, whatever their size and the composition and extent of their communities, are similar in what they try to do and in many of the problems with which they must come to grips, though these may vary from place to place in number, complexity, and magnitude. It is the commonality underlying the small and the large, the simple and the complex, that brings us together on this occasion.

In recent years there have been enormous social, technological, economic, and what might broadly be called bibliographic changes in our society. Libraries of all kinds have had to face a bibliographic record growing in size, in complexity, and in difficulty of access and control. They have had to operate in circumstances of ever more urgent competition for increasingly scarce fiscal and other resources. Under constraints of costs and the manifold difficulties associated with that complex documentary corpus from which selection must be made, libraries of all kinds are being forced to reexamine their roles with respect to their clients and each other and their capabilities for successfully carrying out these roles. They are being forced to question the basic assumptions under which they have operated in the past. They have sought assistance with the problems that press upon them in technology, in new structural arrangements, in approaches to comprehensive planning, and in many other ways.

The public library, no less than any other kind of library, has had to engage in a process of thoughtful examination of those forces which are determining what it can do and what it can become. In a complex and changing environment, how can it be as effective as possible? It is essentially the nature of this question that I wish to deal with here. On the one hand, the question is a substantive one, and we must attempt to answer it. On the other hand, in itself it is not a specifically contemporary question. A form of it is at the root of the gradual but far-reaching evolution that has been occurring in the public library since its inception.

In origin narrowly educational, the objectives of the public library soon broadened to include the provision of informational and recreational services for an increasingly wide range of users. The history of the public library during the last 100 years is characterized by steady growth in the complexity of its organization and in the sophistication of the services it has been able to offer its community. But from its very beginning, in relation to every development that has occurred, there has been vigorous, sometimes acrimonious, debate about the precise nature of the services the library should offer, the best ways of providing them, the appropriate audience to which they should be addressed, and the nature of the library's role vis-à-vis other libraries and other social service and welfare agencies in the community. In my view these debates represent an aspect of a controlled, deliberative adaptation of the public library to the circumstances of the period in which the debate occurred and to the prospects that then seemed to lie before it. They represent historical attempts to answer versions of the question I have posed.

The History of the Public Library: Continuity and Change

In contemplating the history of the public library, one may well be astonished both at the magnitude of the changes that have occurred within it and at the continuity of purposes and functions that can be identified beneath these changes. I would like briefly to explore these notions of continuity and change in the public library. I would like to suggest a view of its development that, while by no means unique, has not been adequately explored because most of its historians have tended to be absorbed by its origins and early history.

The view I would like to suggest is positive and optimistic. It repudiates the pessimistic view often expressed in the literature that the public library is a passive, reactionary, barely viable institution constantly threatened either with obsolescence because of its rigidity and the neglect of local government or with displacement by vital and ingenious private enterprise and more innovative agencies of government. It seems to me that in the course of its history the public library has proved to be a remarkably durable and adaptable organization, in delicate but unceasing interaction with those agencies in its environment the functions of which may complement or conflict with its own. Support for all of these agencies is never fixed but is subject to regular renegotiation rarely concluded to the satisfaction of all.

Evolutionary Changes

What then are some of the changes that have marked this evolutionary process to which I refer? For purposes of argument, let us consider that the prototype mid- to late-nineteenth-century public library was simply an organized collection of high quality, carefully selected, edifying books housed principally in closed-access shelves in an imposing, porticoed building of marble and stone. The collection was intended to assist the self-improvement of those with a sufficiently strong intellectual, social, or economic motivation to try to digest its contents. In the 100 or so years since this library was created, it has attempted to absorb, organize, and rationalize into its collections new kinds of documentary materials. These were materials recognized as having acquired importance because of the development of increasingly complex objectives, a complexity which the existence of these very materials helped to determine. There were popular novels and magazines—the idea of including these in a public library's collection created a furor that began before and lasted beyond the century's turning point. Then, at various times, came films, phonograph records, cassettes, music scores, paperback books, large print books, braille and talking books, art prints, even comics, posters, and so on.

Very soon in its history the library attempted to identify and reach out to special clienteles, to whom it attempted to offer its usual services, specially adapted variants of them, or experimental or new services. Among the first groups for whom special services were offered were children. At various times attempts have been made to reach the working poor, immigrants, the local business community, students, young adults, the disadvantaged, the homebound, the institutionalized, and the elderly.

The library's facilities and equipment have also reflected its evolution. The monumental architecture of the first public libraries and of the later Carnegie libraries, with rigidly prescribed spatial relationships limiting forms of collection organization and service options, has been replaced whenever possible (and when the public librarian's ideal of what is best in design has been achieved) by bright, functional, flexible, comfortable buildings that are attractive and modern without being threatening to the ordinary user.

Continuity of successful changes in the public library has been assured by the development of organizational structure—departments, offices, units, one or more professional and other personnel in appropriately defined and maintained positions. These and the interrelationships among them have themselves gradually been adapted over time as professional views have changed. Moreover, as part of the process of consolidating and testing change has been the emergence of a special literature, from news items about experimental programs and services to monographic reports and textbooks—on the readers' adviser, the administration of county libraries, adult education, public library services to business, and so on. Moreover, almost every development has received institutional expression, and, as time went by, sometimes promotion or demotion, within the American Library Association or state and regional associations—a committee, a round table, a division, or a federated association.

This literature, the structural representation in the ALA, and the administrative and organizational developments in libraries themselves all are products of evolutionary interaction of change and continuity during the course of the public library's history. Underlying them all have been widely shared professional beliefs about the nature of the public library's functions. It is difficult to say when these beliefs formalized, but a major, recognizably modern body of them had crystallized by the 1920s. It is the attempt to give organizational expression to these beliefs that has made the public library a recognizable institution, essentially different from other libraries and related agencies, no matter how similar it may appear to be to them.

Professional Beliefs about Public Library Functions

One such belief was that the collections of the library should be appropriate to a library's particular community and should be as accessible to that community as possible. To this we owe open-access collections (a most controversial step in the nineteenth century, especially in England), the development of concepts of community analysis, and the formulation of local book- and, later, materials-selection policies. To it we also owe various forms of subject-divisional organization of collections and the creation of children's collections and, sometimes, young adult collections. This belief underlies such phenomena as the branch library, the deposit station, the early home library, the bookmobile, and books-by-mail. It has led in the past to the supply of books by wagon and by canoe and sometimes, today, the supply of books by airplane.

Another belief was that the public library should actively provide access to information. What a statement like this implies has always been a subject for debate, but it underlies the creation of telephone reference services, reference departments, business and industry information services, and, most recently, information and referral (I & R) services and the introduction of computer-based bibliographic search services.

Another belief was related to education. From this derived the adult-education activities of the public library so ably studied by Monroe [1] and Lee [2]. Some of these activities, once in the person of a readers' adviser and now in the person of someone called the learners' adviser, are directed toward individuals. Others involve groups, but both orientations have led to much necessary interaction with other community education agencies.

A belief perhaps later in emerging than those just mentioned is that the library should actively mobilize and exploit its resources for its community as a whole or for major portions of it. This has led to various forms of programming: the story hour for children, record evenings, film programs, book and other exhibits, and various kinds of special events. Related to this belief is another: that the library must make its services widely known and their value realized. Interest in public relations emerged in the early part of this century, and was reflected at the time in work of the ALA. There are, of course, two intimately related functions of public relations. One is to influence community support for the library, a necessary and inevitably endless process; the other is to inform the community about and encourage it to use the library's materials and services.

In developing, modifying, abandoning, and reintroducing various institutional expressions of these functions, the public library has always been constrained by the limits of its financial and other resources. These limits have led to different orderings of priorities in services and collection building from library to library. The historical struggle to transcend these limits led to a number of administrative and financial developments, such as the setting up of county libraries in California and elsewhere in the first decades of the century and later, in the 1930s, to the provision of small state grants-in-aid for public libraries. Thus began a pattern of experimentation with ways of achieving a larger tax base to provide support for fuller public library service than was otherwise possible and attempts to obtain special funding for special purposes that are now major phenomena in public library administration. The need for support to set up experimental programs and to explore the ramifications and effectiveness of developments and changes in aspects of organization and services that occurred as a result led to attempts to tap the resources of foundations and of government—the Carnegie Corporation fifty years ago and the U.S. Office of Education and the National Endowment for the Humanities today. The cessation of particular grants, on the one hand, and the results of the surveys and studies of innovations they supported, on the other, have provided critical tests of the relative importance of new developments as compared with established methods in fulfilling the functions I have just identified.

A Perspective for This Conference

This is the perspective I wish to provide for this conference, an awareness of the public library's long history of adaptability and change while maintaining a strong continuity of what I have called characteristic function. My view is that the ability to change that the public library has manifested historically continues to be a source of strength, not a reflection of directionlessness as some would have us believe. Conversely, the continuity that binds our present public library to all of its previous avatars can be considered not a sign of maladaptive rigidity, but of social and professional validation of important functions.

In this conference, we are to engage in that historical process of discussion of the question I posed at the beginning of this paper: In a complex and changing environment, how can the public library be as effective as possible? If we are to assess the present circumstances which shape its future prospects, it seems clear to me that we have to be aware of the cumulative, constantly revised answer to that question as it has been formulated in the past. Any changes we propose in a contemporary answer to it must take place within the framework of that continuity, what one might call that strength of public library tradition, which history is continually testing.

For our own contemporary discussion of the question, itself a historical process as I have attempted to show, it seems to me that first we must attempt to identify and understand the implications of the characteristic circumstances of our own day, what one may call contemporary forces for change, and then we must examine from our own perspectives the existing institutional expression of those functions I described above. These views have influenced the form in which this conference is cast.

Forces for Change and the Conference Papers

It seems to me that among the major distinctly contemporary forces for change there are at least four that should be singled out for exploration. First, the media. Newspapers, magazines, paperback books, radio, and TV have provided us with an educational, recreational, informational, and cultural environment instantly accessible to all at relatively little cost. Immediately one wonders: What has happened to people's information needs in a media-rich environment? How, when, and where do they get information? How and for what purposes do they use the different media? What are the implications of the individual media and of the environment that they together create for the public library, many of the traditional functions of which they seem to have assumed in some way or another? This is the subject of our first paper and, in a sense, sets the broadest possible context for all of the others.

The second major force for change involves the emerging complexity of the role of different levels of government in the fiscal support of public libraries. Here, major questions are: What are the respective roles of local, state, and federal government in supporting public libraries, and what are the consequences for the local agency of increased state and federal involvement? These are aspects of a more general, ever-present question: Where does the public library get its resources? What are the forces that influence the allocation of these resources? What are current and emergent patterns in terms of income and expenditure in the public library? This is the subject of our second paper.

The third major force for change is technology, especially the computer, which has presented libraries with the reality of implementing a range of technical and service options of previously unparalleled scope. But the computer is not the only technological innovation important here, for it is clear that video technology has, or at least was thought to have, implications for public library service, and developments in microphotography and telefacsimile transmission of texts are, or may well become, important. The question, then, most generally put is: To what extent and with what success is the public library attempting to utilize these developments to improve its organization and services? How has the existence and use of modern information technology affected the organizational structure of the public library and the nature and patterns of services offered by it? This is the subject of our third paper.

The fourth major force for change is the contemporary trend toward the formation of networks and systems and larger units of service. The last of these in practice, and as far as the adjurations of the literature go, is not new, for it represents the search for a larger tax base while maintaining the public library's status as a local community agency. In many states nowadays, following the pattern of New York and Illinois, a secondary or supplementary level of public library service—the library system—has been set up. This offers service to libraries in a particular area of a state rather than to the public of a local community. In a number of states the libraries so served were once only public libraries, but the trend now is to involve all kinds of libraries. Other forms of institutionalized multitype library cooperation have become increasingly common. In sum, there is a far-reaching, fragmented, but powerful movement that has been gathering force in the last decade or so toward the integration of certain bibliographic resources and library services locally, regionally, by state, by multistate region, and nationally through networks, consortia, cooperatives, councils, and systems that cut across traditional jurisdictions. In my view, these developments, essentially stemming from early, relatively simple patterns of interlibrary lending and the formation of larger public library units of service, are among the most exciting and problematic that have occurred in recent times, and their existence raises a multitude of questions for the public library. This is the subject of our fourth paper.

These four areas represent especially important contemporary circumstances that will have a bearing on the prospects of the public library. But it is necessary to take a complementary approach. As I indicated earlier, the public library as it currently exists is the product of a long evolution in which certain institutionalized expressions of characteristic functions have been tested, accepted, and incorporated administratively into it. What changes are occurring in these, and toward what ends? The next group of papers examines the traditional information, recreation, and education functions of the public library, and the subject matter has been divided up in a way that is itself traditional—by major user groups: adult, young adult, children. Information services seem so pervasive in the modern public library that they will be treated separately. This artificial division has created problems for our speakers, for the logical distinctions between education, information, and recreation are by no means clear or easy to maintain. Moreover, each of the subjects of the earlier papers—media, finances, technology, and "networking"—impinges on these areas also. We have tried to avoid unnecessary duplication or overlapping in all the papers. This has led to difficult and artificial constraints for all of the contributors who valiantly struggled to keep their papers within the limits assigned them. But as a group, these papers, implicitly acknowledging the continuity of function that I have attempted to describe, assess the circumstances and prospects of so-called traditional library service—traditional not in the sense of orthodox or accepted or common, but in the sense of being a direct, perhaps the most recent institutional expression of the public library's historical functions.

The public library, however, is not merely an American institution. In assessing the present status of the American public library, can we learn from experiences elsewhere, especially where social and cultural backgrounds are, though distinctive, sufficiently similar to make comparison likely to be interesting and fruitful? Our penultimate paper presents an overview of the major circumstances and prospects of British public libraries.

Finally, what can be said of the future of the public library? If we are to risk attempting any answer to our question about making the public library as effective as possible in a changing environment, what can we say is likely to happen to it? What should be done to help to redefine more completely in contemporary terms its complex goals, to realize its traditional strengths in today's society, and to shed or modify whatever from its past seems no longer appropriate or responsive to the needs of its community? This assessment of prospects for change and a summary of the conference forms the basis of the concluding paper.

It should be stressed that the purpose of this conference is not to attempt to provide a blueprint for the future or even to be strongly predictive. The conference is intended to stimulate useful discussion. An important feature of the conferences of the Graduate Library School are the exchanges that take place on the floor between speakers and their audience. This is an immediate and local form of discussion that helps to make the conference occasion a stimulating experience for all participants. Another form of discussion, though more remote, is no less important; it occurs when the papers are read in the published proceedings. Then an audience, more numerous and various than any that can possibly forgather at the University of Chicago's Center for Continuing Education, probes and tests what has been said in the light of its vast experience. Our major purpose, then, is to help inform the judgment of all of those who, working in an enormous range of responsible positions, must make the decisions that cumulatively shape the public library's future. Ultimately, the papers of this conference will form part of the historical record of analysis and review that the public library will leave behind it as it continues to evolve. To have contributed in some measure to the success of this evolution is our aspiration.

REFERENCES

1. Monroe, Margaret E. *Library Adult Education: The Biography of an Idea.* New York: Scarecrow Press, 1963.
2. Lee, Robert Ellis. *Continuing Education for Adults through the American Public Library, 1833–1964.* Chicago: American Library Association, 1966.

THE PUBLIC LIBRARY IN A COMMUNICATIONS SETTING

Gordon Stevenson

Eleven years ago, the Graduate Library School devoted its annual conference to an examination of the public library in the urban setting [1]. At that time we were in the midst of an era of change and uncertainty, and librarians faced many new problems. Most of these problems were intertwined with the structure and dynamics of urban life in a rapidly disintegrating social and economic environment. We knew that the future of the library would be determined to a very large extent by the future of the city. To learn what we could about this urban setting, we turned to urban sociologists, city planners, and students of public affairs. We learned the importance of studying local political processes; the sources and uses of power; the physical disposition of the city's various zones of work and residence, its economic base, its complex cultural and economic ties with suburban areas, the flow of traffic, social stratification, the human ecology of neighborhoods, the sources of intercultural conflict, and demographic structure and trends. The analysis of such phenomena is still essential in library planning. But all urban processes—and, indeed, all social interactions—have one fundamental structural feature in common: they are all formed and maintained by systems of communications.

We can identify three broad categories of communications systems which are necessary to the functioning of any tax-supported public service agency such as the public library. Two of these categories are external, one is internal. Internal systems are managerial, and their purpose is to organize people in order to achieve institutional goals. The external systems influence decisions about what librarians do and how they do it, for they control the environment with which the library must interact. This is an environment of other agencies, institutions, and people. We interact with it at two levels. First, there is the level of governmental bureaucracies (that is, the level at which we interact with city managers, state legislatures, and other formal and informal groups).

It is at this level that we must legitimate our claim to serve the public weal, and here we bargain for economic resources. The other external involvement is with the people to whom we deliver services. These dimensions to communications (which are largely interpersonal) are complicated by mass-media systems which create a larger environment which affects institutions, individuals, and their interrelationships. All of these systems are part of the communications setting of the public library.

In this setting there are systems of political, cultural, and economic communications which control and guide society. There is no way that public library services can fail to be touched by these dynamic social processes. One of the most singular changes in the public library's environment in recent times has been in the relationship between information and the economic system. From a pre–World War II industrial economy, the United States has moved to a service-based economy, which Daniel Bell has characterized as the "post-industrial society" [2]. A unique aspect of this economy is the extent to which it depends on a constant flow of information in order to function. But information is not only the means by which the system operates, it is also a part of the economy; it is a product, a consumer good.

If we define the information industries as all work, goods, and services directly or indirectly related to producing, gathering, manufacturing, processing, handling, storing, and diffusing information, we are talking about an extremely diverse group of industries which in their totality account for almost 50 percent of the gross national product. Approximately the same percentage of the labor force is engaged in these industries [3]. Ithiel de Sola Pool put it this way: "More people in this country now earn their living by manipulating symbols than by making or handling goods" [4, p. 262]. This is without historical precedent. Ours has become an "information society," and no one seems to know what this means in terms of the quality of life—we are, after all, only at the beginning of the age of the computer. But, as de Sola Pool has pointed out, we will all very soon find out what it means [4, p. 263].

It is within this setting that the library must find and implement its social purpose. Whatever that purpose may be, it surely must contribute in some constructive way to the quality of life of the ordinary citizen. In delivering information services, the library changes—even though it may be only to a small degree—the circumstances under which people conduct their lives; it changes their informational environment. To understand the impact, real or potential, of the public library, we must examine the flow of information at the point where it enters the lives of people. To find out what this involves, all we have to do is look around us. We are in the middle of a large and complex communications setting: the city of Chicago.

A Communications Setting[1]

Whatever the people of Chicago are doing right now, it is a safe assumption that few of them are pondering the larger implications of living in a postindustrial society. Most of them are now facing, as we all must, the immediate problems of getting through the day. And in doing this they are almost constantly sending messages, receiving messages, or processing information. Most of these people live in a world they never made and over which they can exercise only a very limited amount of control. How they make out today—whether things go well or badly—will depend very much on the quality of their information sources and their communications skills.

The people of Chicago, and people everywhere else in the United States, have access to massive quantities of information. Much of this information is free, and much of it is relatively inexpensive. In some cases, information of a sort is forced upon people—like that aural wallpaper called Muzak, it is part of the physical environment. Of course, much information is also very expensive, and some of it is quite difficult to get.

In the case of the mass media, people are dealing with one-way systems. Most of what they get free from the mass media is given to them for the sole purpose of changing their behavior. The mass media may inform, instruct, and entertain, but they exist primarily to persuade. It is for this reason, and this reason only, that there are sixty-four radio stations in the Chicago area. Each of these stations is competing with the other sixty-three for its share of the listening audience [6, p. 308]. There are seven television channels in Chicago, and more are brought in on the cable. In their television watching, Chicagoans have relatively few choices. If this city is typical of national norms, 67 percent of local broadcasting schedules are taken from the national networks [7].

Major wire services gather together the news of the world, and teletype machines clamor away day and night. In the newsrooms of local newspapers, editors are sifting through this mass of material. Of the wire-service news they receive, they will select—through a process about which very little is known—between 10 and 20 percent for publication. The events described in the other 80–90 percent will never have happened as far as newspaper readers are concerned [8, p. 90].

Paper and ink are everywhere. Supermarkets, drugstores, and news-stands display thousands of paperback books and magazines. The

1. Chicago, with its complicated systems of communications, deserves more than these brief comments. The city has been the subject of a long series of studies going back to the 1920s, when Robert Park and his colleagues in the Department of Sociology at the University of Chicago pioneered in the study of urban sociology [5, pp. 88–125].

distribution of the bulk of these information sources is governed by rack jobbers and managers of news agencies who monitor sales to decide what will go on the racks tomorrow or next week. The reading of millions of people is determined by these entrepreneurs, and we know practically nothing about them. They are gatekeepers tending the flow of information.

Politicians and government officials are working on news releases, deciding what information will remain secret and what will be sent to the American people. It is not unreasonable to assume that in these decisions they will be guided by their own best interests. They, too, are gatekeepers. In the meantime, dossiers are being compiled and data banks are being searched for credit ratings and past indiscretions. The people of Chicago are being surveyed, counted, categorized, and analyzed. And most of them will never see the results of this survey research.

Chicago sends messages and it receives messages. We hardly need a systematic survey to demonstrate that any city sends fewer messages than it receives. Be that as it may, Chicago—the home of several major publishers and newspaper syndicates—is sending out its share of messages to the rest of the world. This is a top-fifty market. If a local disc jockey broadcasts a popular recording today, and if it sells in quantity tomorrow, it will be broadcast in thousands of other cities in the United States within a few days. And at this very moment Ann Landers may be handing one of her little essays to her copy editor. Very soon the presses will roll and her message will be delivered to millions of people all over the country. Then people will know what to do about problems such as errant wives, wayward husbands, barking dogs, and birth control pills. At least a few of life's little problems will be solved.

Many people would lose interest in reading the daily newspaper if it were not for Ann Landers, the advertisements, the want ads, and the crossword puzzles. In fact, because of the declining readership and shifts in advertising revenue to the electronic media, Chicago has one less newspaper than it did some months ago. More and more, people are depending on television for news of the outside world. One commentator recently wrote that "there are no mass media: all we have is television" [9, p. 17].

But in many respects, the massive size of this city works to the advantage of readers. The best bookstores and the largest libraries have always been in the largest cities. And so it is with Chicago. Despite the inroads of other media during the past quarter-century, the print industries continue to produce large quantities of material [10]. In the United States, the number of books published each year has more than doubled since 1955, although the number of people reporting that reading is one of their "favorite leisure time activities" has declined [11, pp. 492, 516].

With all of these information sources, people still find it necessary, convenient, and even interesting to talk to each other. Most people prefer to talk to people they know. They live within a web of interpersonal relationships which is a major source of information. It has been estimated that any given individual knows between 500 and 2,000 other people [12, p. 119]. But ongoing human contacts on any regular basis outside of a work environment are much more limited. The city has been called "a world of strangers" [13]. It may be that for many people, but for those who live in ethnic neighborhoods it is a world of close personal ties—which is why such residents have been called the "urban villagers" [14]. To talk to people is to be involved in one's human environment.

People cluster together in groups to ward off loneliness and to bring some pattern and meaning to their lives. These groups are held together by systems of communication based on common symbols, shared beliefs, and accepted role structures. It is not always easy for an outsider to penetrate these groups. To an outsider, they sometimes seem pathetic. For example, in Chicago there are a number of "hillbilly bars." In these places, lonely men drink beer and listen to jukeboxes playing recordings of country and western music. The music they listen to was probably recorded in Nashville sometime during the past six months. It has its roots deep in America's rural past, its values are conservative and middle to lower class, and it comments on an intimate world of marriage and family life, love and loneliness, the evils of drink and other human frailties, and sometimes the besetting sins of the city. The lyrics of the songs and the southern regional accents of the singers will remind the men of who they are, what they believe in, and where they came from. The music is very important to them, but to outsiders it is merely quaint or funny.

The social life of Chicago is stratified along racial and socioeconomic lines. And this has a crucial impact on the physical disposition of people. It is not just that people live in different places, but that life for some of them is a fundamentally different experience.

The neighborhood structure of Chicago has fascinated sociologists for more than fifty years. When the city was studied in the 1920s and 1930s, Ernest Burgess identified seventy-five neighborhoods [15, p. 83]. Even today, some of these neighborhoods (with their own traditions and life-styles) are so dissimilar that when residents from different areas interact we can speak of intercultural communications. Within these groups there seem to be general patterns of communication. Nan Lin has observed that "within racially defined networks, communication flow is more effective downward in the status hierarchy . . . and from persons with higher occupational status toward targets of relatively low occupational status . . ." [16, p. 107]. Within groups there are informational elites, and communications between groups are fraught with difficulties.

These and other characteristics of interpersonal communications, though functioning as binding devices for group cohesion, spill over into all aspects of social life, separating people from each other, from their governments, and even from the social institutions which try to serve them.

In branches of the Chicago Public Library, groups of people are talking to each other in twos. In each case, one is a citizen of Chicago and the other is a librarian. More than likely, they are strangers. They may come from different cultural backgrounds, and what is happening in each case is a very complex event. The wrong word, a misunderstood facial expression, an unconscious gesture—anything—could suddenly end all meaningful communication. Both of these people have needs and unique identities, and each sees the world the only way anyone can see it: through his own experiences and his own evaluation of the situation. Many such little dyadic interactions as these, mundane though they may be, are the means by which social life is maintained.[2]

This evening, when work is done, millions of Chicagoans will sit in the semidarkness of their living rooms and take part in a strange national ritual. They will watch television. What they see on their television screens will not be essentially different from what approximately 80 million other Americans will see. If these people conform to national norms, they have 10–20 percent more leisure time than they had ten years ago. This means that they have approximately forty hours of discretionary time once work and household chores are done. Around fifteen hours of this time will be spent with the electronic media [18, p. 217]. Thus, for two or three hours each evening, they will be part of a city of the mind, a place where the difference between fantasy and reality is not always clear, a place populated by stereotypes and suffused with subtle symbols, values, and ideologies. They will all be part of this imaginary world, but for each it will be a different place, a unique structure of his own making. There they will find myth, romance, and adventure, and they will receive messages from places far beyond the city of Chicago.

If they live in the suburbs, they will take time out from watching television to make one extended trip to a shopping center this week. If they have children, this will be a family affair, and all will be able to see the wonders of American manufactured goods on display. And there at the shopping center they may find a chapel in which they can pause in the midst of their shopping to seek spiritual sustenance to carry them through yet another day. There may even be a branch of the public

2. Within the vast literature on interpersonal communications, I have found the works of Erving Goffman to be particularly provocative and useful in thinking about human encounters in public libraries (see especially [17]).

library somewhere in the center. The shopping center which I regularly visit—it is not in Chicago—has, in addition to all of these conveniences, a bank, and next to the center is a large cemetery. I sometimes wonder if this is a coincidence or the latest trend in shopping centers. Depending on the time of the year, at the shopping center one can attend lectures on how to be a better consumer, lose weight, make clothes, cook, and fill out one's income tax forms. And at Christmas, Santa Claus will be there—in person. The American shopping center is the natural home of millions of suburban young people—there is no place else to go in the evening. The suburban shopping center is a beehive of communications activities and a learning center.

These, then, are a few aspects of the communications setting of the public library. Although I have illustrated this setting by commenting on one large urban area, the basic processes of communications are not essentially different in suburban and rural areas.[3] The issue is not the city but the relationship between people and their information sources, wherever they may live.

Questions

What questions should be asked about the communications environment and the information-gathering habits of people in order to find out if there is a place for public library services in their lives? What, if anything, does the public library have to do with the dynamics of social organization and the evolution and structure of life-styles and cultures? Rayward has posed these questions in planning this conference: What are people's information needs in a media-rich society? How, when, where, and why do people get information? What are the trends in publishing, reading, and other media usage in our society? How are various information and communications media perceived and for what purpose accessed?

When we ask such questions as these, we are asking questions about human behavior, its causes and its consequences: Why do some people read, while others do not? Why do children spend so much time watching television? What behavioral changes, if any, result from media experiences? Why do some people seek out political information from

3. For a general theory and method for the systematic analysis of communications in urban areas, see R. L. Meier [19]. The classic work of Vidich and Bensman [20] uses a completely different approach (the subject of research was a rural community) but is a fine example of the complex informational environment within which many small public libraries in the United States must operate.

newspapers, seeing greater credibility in this source than in broadcast journalism?

If there is one thing we have learned from the past thirty-some years of communications research in the United States, it is that it is easier to find out how and where people get information than to find out why they get it and what happens once they do get it.

The Personal Matrix

One point that has emerged in communications research with such consistency that it has the status of a natural law is that people perceive messages selectively and subjectively. In some ways, this is the tragedy of our human perceptual systems, but without this internal filtering system we would probably all quickly go mad. As Khandwalla put it, most people "succeed in seeing the world as coherent" [21, p. 212]. To perceive the world as coherent does not necessarily mean that it is coherent or that one is happy about what one perceives. Rather, one thinks one understands what is happening and strives to find some way of explaining causes and effects. The theory of cognitive dissonance assumes that by and large "people act in ways which are consistent with what they know" [22, p. 17]—with what *they* know, not with what *we* know. Each message is interpreted in the light of the person's internal store of information [23, p. 326]. And, as has been noted, "individuals have stored a lifetime of experiences, some of them positively rewarded, some negatively rewarded, and some unrewarded. The sum total of these experiences has led to the formulation of goals, beliefs, knowledges, self-images, and alternative plans for coping with the environment. This cluster of cognitive elements comprises what we might call an individual's 'image' of reality. On the basis of this image, man interprets his environment and chooses strategies for coping with it" [24, p. 243].

This framework for a consideration of communications behavior is nicely explained by Kurt Lewin's field theory, which posits a finite information field [25]. This is an individual's "life space," the space "containing the individual and his environment. Psychologically, the environment is the environment only as perceived by the individual and in relation to his needs, goals, and purposes . . ." [26, p. 184]. And this, we must remember, is as true of librarians as it is of the people librarians want to serve. It is in the nature of needs, goals, and purposes that much information is completely ignored, some information has to be distorted in order to fit into one's cognitive system, some information is used and quickly forgotten, and other information remains with people the rest of their lives (some of it buried in the depths of the subconscious).

In an effort to explain how this internal system works (that is, how the mind interacts with its informational environment), human beings have been described as "information-processing systems," "decision-making systems," and "problem-solving systems." These mechanical analogies suggest logic and objectivity. But to assume logic and objectivity is to court disaster, as anyone who has administered a library or worked with the public must know. For, as Brenda Dervin reminds us: "Meanings are in the people. People construct their own reality. No knowledge is absolute. Messages sent do not equal messages received. The same person is different across time and space" [23, p. 324].

Needs

To explain the infinite varieties of human behavior, no concept has been more widely propagated than the concept of "needs." Why do people watch television? Because it gratifies some need. However, the term is used very loosely and in two somewhat different meanings. In a psychological sense, needs are what people want (that is, what they know they want, believe they want, or say they want). In its other usage, it is a term to identify what we think other people should want, what we think is good for them, or what we think is good for society.

Properly defined, a need is "any lack or deficiency which is felt by the individual to be inimical to his welfare" [26, p. 313]. People are driven to action by a series of needs which begin with the most basic physical needs and finally culminate in goals which represent the ultimate meaning and purpose of their lives. Physical needs must be gratified in order to sustain life. But above all, people need a purpose in their lives, so we speak of the need for self-actualization, achievement, and success. The gratification of needs, or at least some of them, means nothing outside of some human context, and so there are needs for a sense of belonging and affiliation. Clearly, people need information by which they can find a place in the economic system—what happens at this level will have an influence on the options available to gratify more intangible needs.

In considering the spectrum of human needs and the information sources to which they can be related, it is the complex of lower-level needs which are the easiest to identify. For one thing, the extent to which these needs are gratified is often evident, sometimes glaringly so, in a person's life-style, place of residence, occupation, and income. But long-term goals and higher-level needs only emerge with in-depth interviews, for when a person reveals them, one is given access to private hopes and dreams. No absolute scale is possible by which we can rank these higher-level needs in a way which can be related to the informational needs of all individuals. The definition of success and ways of achieving it have meaning only within a cultural context. And if you and I have aesthetic needs which we gratify by listening to symphonies of Beethoven, I believe it would be a grave mistake to assume that other people can or should gratify their aesthetic needs in the same manner.

Self-Perception of Needs

In considering specific people and specific groups of people, there are several ways we can go about coming to some conclusions about what their information needs are. One way is to ask them. However, people tend to think not in terms of needs but in terms of methods of gratifying needs. For example, a person may say, "I need a new car," but the basic need may be for identity, for visual symbols of status, for self-fulfillment, and possibly even for transportation.

More interesting results emerge when people are asked to identify "problems" which are bothering them. They will usually respond by identifying issues of immediate concern, and these will be of a very practical nature. This was the approach used by Warner when he sampled a cross section of people from various socioeconomic groups in the Baltimore area. One is astonished to learn that 11 percent of the people interviewed either could not or would not identify any problems. Those who did reported an average of four or five problems each. Who had the most problems? The poor? The old? Those in low-status and low-paying jobs? No, none of these. Warner found that the people likely to cite the most problems were "respondents who were young, who were highly educated, those receiving the highest income . . . and those in professional and managerial occupations" [27, p. 2].

The explanation for this striking anomaly is probably to be found in the value systems of working-class people, the poor, and the marginally poor. In her book, *Worlds of Pain*, Rubin examined the lives of working-class people and concluded that these people, with their failures, frustrations, and disillusionments, have been taught to blame themselves for what has happened to their lives. This, Rubin believes, is "a product, at least in part, of the individualistic ethic in the American society which fixes responsibility for any failure to achieve the American dream in individual inadequacy" [28, p. 19].

In order to explain human behavior which does not seem to conform to the traditional American values of dedication to work and to self-improvement, we have invented the concept of "delayed gratification." This, we have assumed, is a trait characteristic of the ambitious and the upwardly mobile person—lazy and unambitious people do not have the willpower to delay immediate gratifications while working and studying to improve themselves. This may be absolute nonsense. Rubin believes that "it is those at the lower ends of the socio-economic order who are forced to delay gratification" [28, p. 75], and more than likely they take these delayed gratifications to the grave with them. In other words, the individual's ranking of needs—wherever that person may be placed in a socioeconomic hierarchy—is conditioned by the individual's perception of his or her ability to affect the environment. In reading a college textbook on consumer behavior, I found several generalizations which seem to explain this human characteristic: "Consumer aspirations tend to grow with achievement. Consumer aspirations are influenced by the performance of other members of the group to which the person belongs. . . . Consumer aspirations are reality oriented . . ." [29, p. 230].[4] To understand the needs of people is to have the ability to control their behavior—to the extent that one has control over the means by which their needs can be gratified.

Society's Values

It is obvious that, in addition to needs as explicitly defined by the people who have them, we must make use of general and objective systems of need classification. The next step after that is to categorize types of information so that needs and information can be related. To take both of these steps quickly and conveniently, we can use the system proposed by the National Commission on Library and Information Science. The commission identified four general classes of needs, all of which can be related to types of information: educational needs, working needs, cultural needs, and leisure-time needs [33, p. xi].[5]

When we define needs in this way (that is, when we decide what people's needs are), we are making certain assumptions. Without necessarily saying that all people do have, say, for example, educational needs,

---

4. The extensive literature on consumer behavior and advertising is a rich source for librarians interested in finding practical information about human needs and motivations. This literature provides fascinating insights into the extent to which advertisers attempt to change human behavior by using behavioral science research—it is all quite relevant to librarians interested in trying to change the information-gathering habits of people. T. S. Robertson's book [30] provides material on such topics as perception and learning, the impact of culture on consumer habits, social class and life-styles, and group processes. This anthology, *Dimensions of Communication* [31], includes many classics from a wide range of communications research areas, including persuasion, advertising, and selling. In working with groups who are culturally or economically deprived, librarians will find R. Perlman's work enlightening [32].
5. The only aspect of this system which is questionable is the inclusion of a separate category for leisure-time needs. Cultural needs (insofar as they can be separated from working and educational needs) are gratified during time when people are not working, for it is only then that they can pursue culture (be it "serious" or popular) [34, p. 219].

we are saying that some people should feel a need for education, that they should have useful options for gratifying such needs, and that if they do so it will be in the best interests of society and for their own welfare. These, then, are not necessarily needs in a psychological sense but value judgments. For example, we know that many people (perhaps as much as 50 percent of the adult population) have a negligible to moderate interest in political information and public-affairs information—they do not feel a need for such information. But one of the accepted values of our society is that people should feel such needs. Indeed, if the political system is to work, a rather large number of people should feel needs for information about the larger issues which affect their lives. Public institutions do indeed serve needs, but their programs are based on value assumptions and democratic ideologies.

The Distribution of Knowledge

To what extent are people's information needs being met by existing agencies? Dervin has summarized the results of research on this question: "In spite of the abundance of information available, citizens are uninformed about public and private resources, facilities, rights, and programs. They are frustrated in their attempts to get information required for everyday problem solving. The brunt of the evidence presents a clear picture of general inability to cope with information needs" [35, p. 20]. How can this situation exist? What has caused it?

For centuries there has been a trend toward a more equitable distribution of information. The gap separating the information rich from the information poor has slowly narrowed. In order to consider the nature of this trend today, I will make a distinction between the mechanical diffusion of information and the information which people acquire as part of their cognitive systems (that is, knowledge, a body of information-processing skills, and concepts).

There is general agreement among communications researchers that everyone in our society has more information today (compared with, say, thirty years ago). However, the knowledge gap not only remains with us, it is getting larger rather than smaller. This is an unanticipated effect of modern communications technologies. Katzman has developed several hypotheses relevant to this issue: "With the adoption of a new communication technology, people who already have high levels of information and ability will gain more than people with lower initial levels" [36, p. 50]. "New communication techniques and technologies create new information gaps before old gaps close" [ibid., p. 53]. "The widening gap tends to be associated with initial economic and/or informational status more clearly than it is associated with personal ability" [ibid., p. 55].

The knowledge gap exists, and will probably continue to exist, because all—quite literally *all*—of the social, psychological, political, cultural, and economic conditions conducive to the acquisition of new knowledge are more likely to be part of the environment of those who already have a large share of the currently available knowledge. Note that people who are already the most deprived in terms of knowledge are also the heaviest users of the most pervasive mass media. And, as Robinson has noted: "Like almost every other institution in society, abundant evidence suggests that the mass media tend to reinforce and accentuate existing conditions rather than promote egalitarianism or abrupt change, at least with regard to information diffusion. The evidence is persuasive and pervasive that persons already well informed are more motivated to become better informed through the mass media than persons less well informed" [37, p. 87]. This phenomenon has also been noted in the field of adult education. People with the least amount of formal education are the least likely participants in adult education programs [38, p. 248].

Katzman sees the problem in technological terms and writes that "in an urban technological society, the difference between those with and those without access to new communication and information-handling devices often produce the difference between a group that controls its own affairs and a group that is totally dependent on the paternalistic benevolence of the information handlers" [36, p. 53].

As important as information-processing devices may be, the allocation of human resources in the public management of information seems to me to be even more important. Robinson has noted that between 1960 and 1970 there was a "78 percent increase in knowledge producers (researchers and professors) . . . [and a] 55 percent increase in knowledge disseminators (teachers and media specialists)" [18, p. 209]. The producers of knowledge are beginning to outnumber the disseminators of knowledge. This may have more serious consequences than would at first seem evident. The "paternalistic benevolence" may in time be directed to an ever-widening circle of American citizens. It is one thing if the poor get poorer and the rich get richer. It is quite another thing when there are both qualitative and quantitative changes in the two broad categories.

These general problems in the distribution of knowledge may be summarized as follows. (1) There is clearly a large segment of the population which, in relative terms, is poverty stricken in terms of information (we do not know how large it is, and its size depends on the types of information we are talking about—it surely ranges from 20 to 50 percent of the adult population). (2) There are some types of information which are tending to become concentrated in a relatively small part of the population, principally government officials and managers. (3) It appears that on the whole people are getting less information about the politics and governmental activities which affect their lives.

Some of these issues are directly related to what C. Wright Mills wrote about twenty-five years ago in his book, *The Power Elite* [39]. There is no single power elite controlling all channels of communications which serve the American people. But everywhere there are gatekeepers— forces which channel information on its way, divert it, alter it, or stop its flow. The specific goals of gatekeepers may be to control or influence political, economic, or cultural behavior.[6]

Advertising as Gatekeeping

I have already mentioned several types of gatekeepers (newspaper editors, news-agency managers), but the most pervasive gatekeeping system is built into the structure of the broadcasting industries. I am, of course, referring to the institution of advertising.

While librarians are trying to reach people, trying to define and serve their needs, advertising agencies are creating needs, shaping the world, and changing the very fabric of our lives. In doing this, they have the services of the behavioral sciences, control over the electronic media, and very clear and unequivocal goals. For all practical purposes, they are unrestrained in their activities. It is a problem for which I see no immediate answer. As David Potter pointed out, advertisers have created a new and powerful cultural institution, which in its ability to socialize us can be compared with traditional institutions of socialization. He writes: "Advertising has in its dynamics no motivation to seek the improvement of the individual or to impart qualities of social usefulness.... And, though it wields an immense social influence, comparable to the influence of religion and learning, it has no social goals and no social responsibility for what it does with its influence ..." [44, p. 177].

This enterprise involves an investment of well over $25 billion each year, and its only purpose is to change or control human behavior. It is not the advertisements as such which have the most far-reaching cultural consequences but the impact of program content which is now almost exclusively in the hands of the advertisers.

In considering the role of gatekeepers in areas of cultural informa- tion, we have to recognize the fact that one of the most salient features of

6. For a survey of recent gatekeeping research, see Donohue, Tichenor, and Olien [40]. Barnouw's recent book [41] comments on the impact of advertising on television content. George views with considerable concern the use of computerized data banks in controlling society [42]. Bogart reviews the whole area of research in the management of media and outlines an agenda of needed research [43].

modern life is that culture is an industry. Culture is created, manufactured, distributed, and sold in a highly competitive market. Entrepreneurs engaged in this industry make every effort to control their
environment [45]. By and large, I suspect that most of the controls they
use or attempt to use are not deliberately sinister or cynical (but this is a
matter of debate [46, pp. 115–33]). From the point of view of marketing
theory, selling soap is not essentially different from selling recordings of
Beethoven's symphonies. And I suppose there is no moral or legal
reason why there should be a difference.

Acquiring Information

Given these numerous limitations and possibilities, how do people
acquire information? Most research directed to answering this question
has examined the flow of technical, scientific, economic, and professional
information. How people go about acquiring information not related to
their work has received little attention until quite recently [27, 35, 47].

Of the various factors which have some bearing on this question, the
most obvious one is that of physical access. But physical access is not
enough, for the use of various media of communications requires certain
skills by the user. To have access to the largest store of information
requires the ability to read—the more sophisticated the reading ability,
the wider the range of information sources available. This skill is so basic
that the stubborn persistence of functional illiteracy and the continuing
decline in reading ability among the young (which has been documented
for at least fourteen years [48]) is a catastrophe and a disgrace.[7]

Given that sources are physically available and that people can deal
with them, the option to use or not use a source may be determined by
economic factors—it may cost more than the potential user is willing or
able to pay. Furthermore, in order to gratify some information needs,
the individual may have to spend a great amount of time or effort, while
other needs may be gratified quite easily with no more effort than sitting
in front of a television screen. Here we are dealing with an issue which
B. C. Vickery raised when he asked his students of information science
to comment on the proposition that "the design of any information

---

7. Who reads and who does not are important questions, but perhaps more important is
the question of what happens when people do read. Holland's work is representative of
a new area of research into the extent to which different readers interpret the same text
differently [49]. Other skills which are important in the efficient functioning of an
individual's information-gathering system are the ability to receive and process information delivered aurally and to deal with nonalphabetic visual information—the term
"visual literacy" is in common use, and Arnheim speaks of "visual thinking" [50].

service should be predicated on the assumption that its customers will exert minimal effort in order to receive its benefits" [51, p. 235]. If cost and convenience are important factors in information seeking, then the cheapest and most efficient sources are those closest at hand: the mass media and other people.

There is a considerable amount of information available on the amount of time people spend using different media. Some of this information is provocative but leaves many questions unanswered. For example, Harrington wrote that "by the time a person is fourteen, he will witness 18,000 murders on the [television] screen. He will also see 350,000 commercials. By the time he is eighteen, he will stockpile nearly 17,000 hours of viewing experiences, and will watch at least 20 movies for every book he reads. Eventually, the viewing will absorb ten years of his life" [52, p. v]. Millions of dollars are being spent in trying to find out what the information acquired during this lifetime of television watching does to the individual and to society—to date, all results seem inconclusive insofar as solid scientific evidence is concerned. Analyzing content to determine what happens when people interact with message-delivery systems has some limitations. In his critique of television, Mander reviews research on its neurophysiological effects and concludes that "very little cognitive, recallable, analyzable, thought-based learning takes place" [46, p. 205]. Krugman, basing his research on a computer analysis of brain-wave frequency rates, is convinced, with Marshall McLuhan, that "television does not appear to be communication as we have known it" [53, p. 8].

Research in media usage consistently shows a correlation between socioeconomic variables and the time spent with different media. Although almost everyone watches television, those in lower socioeconomic categories spend the most time with it, give it a credibility as high or higher than print sources, and apparently use it as a source for a wide variety of types of information. These same classes generally spend more time listening to radio than others. The limitation in data such as this is that the emphasis is almost always on between-group variance rather than within-group variance. In other words, some people in lower socioeconomic classes do read and read widely, while some people in high socioeconomic classes read very little. Thus for structuring public policy, if it is to improve the information-gathering habits of people, we need many detailed studies of within-group variance—and Wright's work is a solid foundation for this research [54].

This is not to say that a knowledge of between-group variance is not useful. In a comparative study of the information-gathering habits of residents of three different communities in the Los Angeles area, the between-group variance was more extensive than was expected. The researchers felt that their study was persuasive enough to conclude that "in any type of objective management of communication to the public, an agency must take into account quite drastic differences in information sources. No practical attempts to improve the availability of information in a society can be complete unless we know also how, or if, the information will be used" [55, p. 99]. They found such differences as this: in acquiring information about health, in one community 61 percent of the residents turned to the family, but in another community only 2 percent turned to the family and 69 percent turned to municipal agencies. The density of a person's human relationships seems to have some influence on the extent to which there is a dependence on the mass media [56], but people in all occupations and in all socioeconomic groups consistently turn to friends and colleagues for information—for example, it has been claimed that "informal communication accounts for about 80 percent of information transfer amongst research scientists" [57, p. 56]. Frequently consulted persons become the "information elite" [58].

It is obvious that much information is acquired quite randomly while other information is sought out deliberately. Sources of information can be categorized by the way people use them. Patrick Wilson identifies three categories of sources: monitor systems, advisory systems, and reserve systems. We all constantly monitor our environment to "keep our internal model of the world up to date" [59, p. 36]. We use the advisory system for specific information. The reserve system consists of "sources irregularly or never used but still known to be available for use" [59, p. 37].[8] Such categories are not essentially different from Warner et al.'s systems of "ends" and "means" information [27], Atkin's "extrinsic" and "intrinsic" methods of information seeking [60], and Downs's "entertainment information" and "information for decision-making" [61, p. 215]. The purpose of these categories is to provide a functional approach to the use of personal and mass-media sources [62]. The main point is that any given medium or source may serve different functions in the lives of different people.

Conclusions

Where does the public library fit into the communications environment of modern life? In order to answer this question librarians will have to begin with the four categories of needs identified by the National Commission on Libraries and Information Science: educational, occupa-

8. Patrick Wilson thoroughly examines all aspects of the relationship between individuals and their communications environments. His work is bound to have an impact on any serious consideration of public-information policy.

tional, cultural, and leisure-time needs [33, p. xi]. Once needs are identified, a series of questions must be asked about each of them. (1) What system or systems exist to gratify this need? (2) What happens when the gratification of this need is left to the free-enterprise system? (3) How important is this information need, why, and to whom is it important? (4) Why should a public agency intervene in the diffusion process to supply an alternative source of need gratification at public expense?

I am not at all sure that these questions can be asked in general terms. Rather, they should be asked about the information needs of different groups of people (such as the young, the old, the poor, the working and middle classes, etc.).

Our most intractable problem is raised by the last question: Why should the public library respond to information needs? This question cannot be considered independently of other aspects of our socioeconomic system. One purpose of a democratic form of government is to provide people with the maximum opportunity to gratify their needs. This is done by an economic system. We assume that if the means for gratifying needs are left to the free competitive market, all will work out well in the end. Everyone will get his fair share, which is what he is able to pay for (that is, each person puts into the system the equivalent of what is taken out of the system). The government intervenes (or should intervene) in the system if it does not work or if it results in an injustice [63]. Thus, we have various welfare systems and programs for the unemployed.

There are other obvious cases where the government gets involved in the system. These result in what are called "public goods" and "merit goods" [64]. These are products or services which are either essential to society or enhance it in ways which are not possible if they are left to the free-market system of supply and demand. Some of these goods and services may be provided to a relatively few people, but it is assumed that they have "spinoffs" or "externalities" which are beneficial to society. Free public education through twelve years of schooling is a case in point—and, of course, it has frequently been argued that the use of the public library by 20 percent of the population produces externalities which affect a much larger segment of the population. This is obviously much more complicated than my few brief comments would indicate, for there is a wide range of public goods as diverse as national defense and public parks. But the point is that information is diffused commercially as a product (that is, books are sold) and as a service (such as those information services provided by a lawyer). Why, then, should information, or some information, be taken out of the economic system? In order for something to be taken out of the economic system there must be good and sufficient reason. Obviously, it would be self-defeating if all means of gratifying needs were taken off the market and supplied by the government.

It is with considerable reluctance that I have come to the conclusion that several recent statements which have addressed this issue are not realistic (though it is possible that they were not meant to be).[9] For example, consider the implications of this statement, from a report of an ALA committee charged with outlining a national information policy: "*All information* must be available to *all* people in *all* formats, purveyed through *all* channels and delivered to *all* levels of comprehension" [68, p. 718, emphasis added]. If it is to be the function of the public library to supply all information in all formats to all citizens, we are not promoting library or information policy, we are advocating some new form of socioeconomic structure. I am not sure what this structure would be (and, indeed, it might be a better or more humane system than the one in which we now live), but it would not be a democracy as we know it. If such a system were to operate at maximum efficiency, large segments of the information industry would be in shambles. This is not going to happen, we know it is not going to happen, and I am not even sure we would want it to happen.

This does not mean that there is not a place for the public library in modern life. It does mean we have to be very cautious in competing with existing commercial delivery systems. We intervene in the system when it does not work. And the commercial system can break down at different points—which is to say that for some reason people are not getting the information they want, the information to which they have a legal right, or the information they should want if they are to be responsible members of society. Here are the sorts of problems which might come up in different systems currently diffusing information to the public. (1) There may be problems of content: the content may not be what people need or it may be socially dysfunctional. (2) There may be something wrong with the delivery system; that is, the right information may be available but it is not getting channeled to the people who need it. (3) The fault may lie with the individual; that is, the person's perception of what information is needed may be wrong. (4) And, of course, the needed information may be available, but the individual may be cut off from it by psychological or cultural barriers.

It has been demonstrated that there are areas of real information needs which, for one reason or another, are not being met or are being

9. I am referring to parts of *A Strategy for Public Library Change* [65, p. 46] and the Public Library Association's recent "Mission Statement" [66]. Although these are valuable sources, I am inclined to believe that Feldman was correct in her "unevaluated hunch" that librarians, or some of them, are "acutely self-conscious and overly articulate about philosophy and lofty ideals, and less clear about practical details, realizable aims and methods of attainment" [67, p. 395].

served badly by current commercial delivery systems. In the case of the sorts of information being supplied by information and referral centers, we are dealing with information to which people have a right and which governments have a responsibility to supply without cost. In considering different types of educational, cultural, and occupational information, librarians should make a distinction between problems which can be identified as resulting from a malfunction in a potentially efficient system and those which are the result of the intrinsic structure of the system. For example, major problems exist in the distribution of books and periodicals through commercial outlets. In addition to the problems of the existence of millions of out-of-print books, the provision of commercial access to in-print materials is notoriously inefficient from the point of view of the potential purchaser. But to make the system efficient for the purchaser (that is, display massive stocks of material on all subjects) would create an economically inefficient system for publishers. Thus, one can justify the provision of such materials in public libraries.

But of all possible problems which may come up in considering the commercial delivery systems, none has more significance for public-library policy than the extent to which the flow of information is controlled by various systems of gatekeeping. The public library and its services can be justified to the extent that they serve as channels through which information—otherwise inaccessible—will become available to the American people. We may live in a media-rich society, but in fact very little of those riches are available to any single person. Most of what people get is presented by the managers of the mass media, and Herbert Schiller wrote that "America's media managers create, process, refine, and preside over the circulation of images and information which determine our beliefs and attitudes and, ultimately, our behavior" [69, p. 1].

After having considered the vastness of current communications systems and the high concentration of power in the hands of a relatively few managers, I am convinced that, far from being a nineteenth-century anachronism, the public library has never had a more important role to play in the diffusion of information.

REFERENCES

1. Carnovsky, Leon, ed. *The Public Library in the Urban Setting.* The Thirty-second Conference of the Graduate Library School, July 31–August 2, 1967. Chicago: University of Chicago Press, 1968.
2. Bell, Daniel. *The Coming of Post-industrial Society.* New York: Basic Books, 1973.
3. Porat, Marc Uri. *The Information Economy.* ED 142 205-13. 9 vols. Washington, D.C.: U.S. Department of Commerce, Office of Telecommunications, 1977.

4. De Sola Pool, Ithiel. "Technology and Policy in the Information Age." In *Communication Research: A Half-Century Appraisal,* edited by Daniel Lerner and Lyle M. Nelson. Honolulu: University Press of Hawaii, 1977.
5. Madge, John. *The Origins of Scientific Sociology.* New York: Free Press, 1962.
6. Owen, Bruce M. "Regulating Diversity: The Case of Radio Formats." *Journal of Broadcasting* 21 (Summer 1977): 305–19.
7. Bedell, Sally. "TV Update." *TV Guide* 26, no. 11 (March 18, 1978): A 1–2.
8. Bagdikian, Ben H. *The Information Machines: Their Impact on Men and the Media.* New York: Harper & Row, 1971.
9. Schrank, Jeffrey. *Snap, Crackle, and Popular Taste.* New York: Delta Books, 1977.
10. Grannis, Chandler B. "1977: The Year in Review." *Publishers Weekly* 213, no. 8 (February 20, 1978): 65–71.
11. U.S. Department of Commerce. Office of Federal Statistical Policy and Standards. *Social Indicators: 1976.* Washington, D.C.: Government Printing Office, 1977.
12. Davison, W. Phillips; Boylan, James; and Yu, Frederick T. C. *Mass Media: Systems and Effects.* New York: Praeger Publishers, 1976.
13. Lofland, Lyn H. *A World of Strangers: Order and Action in Urban Public Space.* New York: Basic Books, 1973.
14. Gans, Herbert. *The Urban Villagers.* New York: Free Press, 1962.
15. Suttles, Gerald D. *The Social Construction of Communities.* Chicago: University of Chicago Press, 1972.
16. Lin, Nan; Dayton, Paul; and Greenwald, Peter. "The Urban Communication Network and Social Stratification: A 'Small World' Experiment." In *Communication Yearbook,* vol. 1, edited by Brent D. Ruben. New Brunswick, N.J.: Transaction Books, 1977.
17. Goffman, Erving. *Frame Analysis.* New York: Harper & Row, 1974.
18. Robinson, John P. " 'Massification' and Democratization of the Leisure Class." *Annals of the American Academy of Political and Social Science* 435 (January 1978): 206–25.
19. Meier, Richard L. *A Communications Theory of Urban Growth.* Cambridge, Mass.: M.I.T. Press, 1962.
20. Vidich, Arthur J., and Bensman, Joseph. *Small Town in Mass Society.* Princeton, N.J.: Princeton University Press, 1968.
21. Khandwalla, Pradip N. *The Design of Organizations.* New York: Harcourt Brace Jovanovich, 1977.
22. Festinger, Leon. "The Theory of Cognitive Dissonance." In *The Science of Human Communication,* edited by Wilbur Schramm. New York: Basic Books, 1963.
23. Dervin, Brenda. "Strategies for Dealing with Human Information Needs: Information or Communication." *Journal of Broadcasting* 20 (Summer 1976): 324–33.
24. Donohew, Lewis, and Tipton, Leonard. "A Conceptual Model of Information Seeking, Avoiding, and Processing." In *New Models for Communication Research,* edited by Peter Clarke. Sage Annual Reviews of Communication Research, vol. 2. Beverly Hills, Calif.: Sage Publications, 1972.
25. Lewin, Kurt. *Field Theory in Social Science.* New York: Harper & Bros., 1951.
26. Chaplin, J. P. *Dictionary of Psychology.* New York: Dell Publishing Co., 1968.
27. Warner, E. S.; Murray, A. D.; and Palmour, V. E. *Information Needs of Urban Residents.* ED 088 464. Final report from Regional Planning Council of Baltimore and Westat, Inc., of Rockland, Md., to the U.S. Department of Health, Education, and Welfare, Office of Education, Division of Library Programs, under contract no. OEC-0-71-455, December 1973.
28. Rubin, Lillian Breslow. *Worlds of Pain: Life in the Working-Class Family.* New York: Basic Books, 1976.
29. Walters, C. Glenn. *Consumer Behavior, Theory and Practice,* 3d ed. Homewood, Ill.: Richard D. Irwin, Inc., 1978.

30. Robertson, Thomas S. *Consumer Behavior.* Glenview, Ill.: Scott, Forseman & Co., 1970.
31. Richardson, Lee, ed. *Dimensions of Communication.* New York: Appleton-Century-Crofts, 1969.
32. Perlman, Robert. *Consumers and Social Services.* New York: John Wiley & Sons, 1975.
33. National Commission on Libraries and Information Science. *Toward a National Program for Library and Information Services: Goals for Action.* Washington, D.C.: Government Printing Office, 1975.
34. **Stevenson, Gordon. "Popular Culture and the Public Library." In *Advances in Librarianship*, vol. 7, edited by Melvin J. Voigt. New York: Academic Press, 1977.**
35. Dervin, Brenda. "The Everyday Information Needs of the Average Citizen: A Taxonomy for Analysis." In *Information for the Community,* edited by Manfred Kochen and Joseph C. Donohue. Chicago: American Library Association, 1976.
36. Katzman, Nathan. "The Impact of Communication Technology: Promises and Prospects." *Journal of Communication* 24, no. 4 (Autumn 1974): 47–58.
37. Robinson, John P. "Mass Communication and Information Diffusion." In *Current Perspectives in Mass Communication Research,* edited by F. Gerald Kline and Phillip J. Tichenor. Sage Annual Reviews of Communication Research, vol. 1. Beverly Hills, Calif.: Sage Publications, 1972.
38. Douglah, Mohammad, and Moss, Gwenna. "Differential Participation Patterns of Adults of Low and High Educational Attainment." *Adult Education Journal* 18 (1968): 247–59.
39. Mills, C. Wright. *The Power Elite.* New York: Oxford University Press, 1956.
40. Donohue, George A.; Tichenor, Phillip J.; and Olien, Clarice N. "Gatekeeping: Mass Media Systems and Information Control." In *Current Perspectives in Mass Communication Research,* edited by F. Gerald Kline and Phillip J. Tichenor. Sage Annual Reviews of **Communication Research, vol. 1. Beverly Hills, Calif.: Sage Publications, 1972.**
41. Barnouw, Erik. *The Sponsored Air.* New York: Oxford University Press, 1978.
42. George, Frank. *Machine Takeover.* Oxford: Pergamon Press, 1978.
43. Bogart, Leo. "The Management of Mass Media." In *Mass Communication Research: Major Issues and Future Directions,* edited by W. Phillips Davison and Frederick T. C. Yu. New York: Praeger Publishers, 1974.
44. Potter, David M. *People of Plenty.* Chicago: University of Chicago Press, 1954.
45. Hirsch, Paul M. "Processing Fads and Fashions: An Organizational-Set Analysis of Cultural Industry Systems." *American Journal of Sociology* 77 (January 1972): 639–59.
46. Mander, Jerry. *Four Arguments for the Elimination of Television.* New York: William Morrow & Co., 1978.
47. **Parker, Edwin B., and Paisley, William J. *Patterns of Adult Information Seeking.* ED 010** 294. Stanford, Calif.: Stanford University, Institute of Communications Research, 1966.
48. " 'Traumas' Blamed for Low College Test Scores." *Knickerbocker News* (August 23, 1977), p. 1.
49. Holland, Norman N. *5 Readers Reading.* New Haven, Conn.: Yale University Press, 1975.
50. Arnheim, Rudolf. *Visual Thinking.* London: Faber & Faber, 1969.
51. Vickery, B. C. *Techniques of Information Retrieval.* London: Butterworth & Co., 1970.
52. Harrington, John. *Rhetoric of Film.* New York: Holt, Rinehart & Winston, 1973.
53. Krugman, Herbert E. "Brain Wave Measures of Media Involvement." *Journal of Advertising Research* 11 (February 1971): 3–9.
54. Wright, Charles R. "Social Structure and Mass Communications Behavior." In *The Idea of Social Structure, Papers in Honor of Robert K. Merton,* edited by Lewis A. Coser. New York: Harcourt Brace Jovanovich, 1975.

55. Williams, Frederick; Dordick, Herbert S.; and Horstmann, Frederick. "Where Citizens Go for Information." *Journal of Communication* 27 (Winter 1977): 95–99.

56. Beinstein, Judith. "Friends, the Media, and Opinion Formation." *Journal of Communication* 27 (Autumn 1977): 30–39.

57. Platt, John. "Information Networks for Human Transformation." In *Information for Action: From Knowledge to Wisdom*, edited by Manfred Kochen. New York: Academic Press, 1975.

58. Wilson, Pauline. *A Community Elite and the Public Library*. Westport, Conn.: Greenwood Press, 1977.

59. Wilson, Patrick. *Public Knowledge, Private Ignorance: Toward a Library and Information Policy*. Westport, Conn.: Greenwood Press, 1976.

60. Atkin, Charles. "Instrumental Utilities and Information Seeking." In *New Models for Communication Research*, edited by Peter Clarke. Sage Annual Reviews of Communication Research, vol. 2. Beverly Hills, Calif.: Sage Publications, 1972.

61. Downs, Anthony. *An Economic Theory of Democracy*. New York: Harper & Row, 1957.

62. Wright, Charles R. "Functional Analysis and Mass Communication." In *People, Society, and Mass Communications*, edited by Lewis Anthony Dexter and David Manning White. New York: Free Press, 1964.

63. Arrow, Kenneth J. "The Effects of the Price System and Market on Urban Economic Development." In *Urban Processes as Viewed by the Social Sciences*, edited by William Gorham. Washington, D.C.: Urban Institute, 1970.

64. Tiebout, Charles M., and Willis, Robert J. "The Public Nature of Libraries." In *The Public Library and the City*, edited by Ralph W. Conant. Cambridge, Mass.: M.I.T. Press, 1965.

65. Public Library Association. *A Strategy for Public Library Change: Proposed Public Library Goals: Feasibility Study*. Allie Beth Martin, Project Coordinator. Chicago: Public Library Association, American Library Association, 1972.

66. Public Library Association. Goals, Guidelines, and Standards Committee. "A Mission Statement for Public Libraries. Guidelines for Public Library Service: Part I." *American Libraries* 8 (December 1977): 615–20.

67. Feldman, Nancy C. "Commentary." *Library Trends* 22 (January 1974): 395–401.

68. Berry, John. "U.S. Info Policy." *Library Journal* 103, no. 7 (April 1, 1978): 718.

69. Schiller, Herbert I. *The Mind Managers*. Boston: Beacon Press, 1973.

THE FINANCIAL SETTING OF THE PUBLIC LIBRARY

R. Kathleen Molz

"Whatever future form government may take, whatever distribution of wealth or social order may prevail, the search for knowledge will inhere in mankind. Government, economic and other systems, may change and with them the public library may have to change method of support and method of service, but undoubtedly the need for its functions will remain. Its service is the very essence of governmental functions and obligation in a democracy, which can go forward only as education spreads. Is the library worthy of support during a depression?" [1, p. 3]. Thus did Carl Vitz pose the fundamental question in a book published during the great economic depression of the 1930s and entitled, not without relevance to the subject of this paper, *Current Problems in Public Library Finance*. Over forty years in time separate us from that earlier period, but it is only with a sense of *déjà vu* that one reexamines some of the chapter headings of Vitz's anthology: "Shrinkage of Public Revenues," "Stretching the Library Dollar," and "Winning Support." Yet, although the feeling that we have all been there before still obtains, a substantive difference distinguishes our problems from those experienced by our 1930s colleagues. Disheartened by a shrinking economy, forced to accept budget cuts and, in some cases, reduced salaries, our predecessors at least could derive some comfort in the realization that their services were being used and used extensively.

R. L. Duffus's short monograph, *Our Starving Libraries* [2], portrays rightly the curious situation prevailing during the depression in which circulation of books and usage of libraries escalated while budgets were being slashed and stringent economies were being introduced. In recalling the public library of his childhood, Langston Hughes once reflected that its attraction lay not only in its silence, big chairs, and long tables, but also in "the fact that the library was always there and didn't seem to have a mortgage on it, or any sort of insecurity about it . . ." [3, p. 26]. I do not know what inner-city children in Newark or New York, St. Louis or Baltimore feel about the public library of today, but I can speculate that they may be growing up with the distinct impression that there is a rather large mortgage on it, one that seems to be growing more burdensome every year.

34

Another factor also seems to differentiate our problems from those of the 1930s. If the old adage is true that misery likes company, then indeed the depression generation of library directors could have at least taken some solace from one another. The depression was a great leveler, and no one engaged in public services was really exempt from its economic fallout. That same situation does not prevail today; the plight of the public libraries in the northeastern corridor and in some midwestern states, once the pride of the public library movement, must be contrasted with developments in growth areas of the country in such municipalities as Houston, Dallas, Albuquerque, and Atlanta where new central libraries have either been built recently or are now being planned. Expansion in the suburbs is evident also in, to name but a few states, Maryland, New York, and Illinois, where suburban systems, created in the postwar era, have greatly expanded, in some cases outdistancing by far both in circulation and in on-site use the cities which once dominated the record of public library performance within the states.

Running counter, then, to declining patterns of library patronage in cities which demonstrated high use during the depression are regions of new growth, particularly in the sun-belt states and in the suburban clusters surrounding the major cities, many of them now deeply mired in a continuing fiscal crisis. So often treated as a distinctive social institution drawing on the local property tax for its principal support, the public library cannot be viewed as an integer but must be seen as an agency responsive to and conditioned by varying economic, demographic, geographic, and social characteristics, all of which can accelerate public library development within a given community, or contribute to its stabilization, or unfortunately lead to its decline. Part of the difficulty in assessing the financial setting of the public library in the United States lies in the simple fact that there is no single setting but rather a plurality of settings which in some regions induce growth and expansion while in others contribute to the library's deterioration and decay.

National Economic Trends

At the same time, the public library must also be viewed within the macrocosmic setting of national economic trends—trends that affect all Americans as taxpayers and contributors to the national income. In his introduction to *Economic Power Failure: The Current American Crisis*, Sumner M. Rosen summarizes the burdens of the national economy of the mid-1970s: escalating oil costs, rising food prices and the virtual disappearance of food surpluses, high mortgage rates with their effect on home construction, the devaluation of the dollar and floating rates of exchange, continuing unemployment especially among ethnic minorities and youth, and the lack of effective government regulation and control over the increasing number of multinational corporations [4, pp. 1–44]. Translated into more mundane terms, all of this means that many Americans are worried about their fuel bills, feel the pinch when groceries have to be purchased, wonder if the next pay raise will even moderately assuage the inflated costs of the goods and materials they use, and buy their gas, perhaps, from a friendly Shell dealer without any consciousness that 69 percent of the Shell Oil Company in this country is owned by its parent conglomerates, the Royal Dutch/Shell group, which has offices in both London and The Hague.

Although today's economy seems to be making some slight recovery from the severe recession of 1975, the long-range forecast is still unclear. In the public sector of the economy, the issues of tax cuts for both individuals and corporations are being examined, but even if relief is held out through these measures, the increase in social security payments and the anticipation that taxes may have to be levied on energy consumption may result in a Pyrrhic victory for the American taxpayer. You may inquire, What does all of this have to do with the financial picture of the public library? I can only suggest that you reread Harry M. Lydenberg's presidential address before the American Library Association in 1933. How, he asked, can financial respite be obtained for the public library when it was the taxpayer himself who needed the relief? The topic of his address, I might add, was "Unanswered Questions," and it is to those still recurring questions that these remarks are addressed.

State Contributions: Schools and Libraries

Historically, in this country the property tax, regarded by many economists as a regressive tax, has been the primary base of public library support. Until this decade, a similar situation prevailed for the nation's public educational system. Since 1971, however, the year marking the *Serrano* v. *Priest* decision in California, twenty-four states have enacted legislation to equalize school districts deriving their income from low property values with those which base them on higher ones. Other states have similar legislation under consideration. Although an assessment of this drastic change in the pattern of school financing may be premature, Edward B. Fiske, education editor of the *New York Times,* provided a useful summary of school finance reform in November 1977. Fiske noted that fourteen states have experienced legislated changes in school financing over a three- to five-year period. According to Fiske and other sources of evaluation which he cited, school finance reform has in general lowered property taxes. "From 1971 to 1975," he wrote, "the average school-tax bite dropped from $26.76 to $24.44 for every $1,000 of personal income, a decline of 9 percent. In the 14 states with the most experience with finance reform, the average drop from 1971 to 1975 was about 24 percent, or nearly three times the national average" [5, p. 1]. Pointing to the nationwide trend of the states' greater assumption of local educational financing, Fiske noted that the trend is strongest in the states adopting reform: "In the 14 states with the most experience with new finance laws, the state share of education costs rose on the average from 43 to 51 percent in the first year" [p. 22]. In the aggregate, the states' share of local school costs rose from 43.1 percent in 1971 to 47.2 in 1976, exclusive of federal funds. In commenting on the effect of financial reform on educational quality, Fiske could only conclude that "there is little evidence one way or the other" [p. 22], adding, however, that states, such as Florida or New Jersey, which legislated the tax changes with other reform measures might have greater success in achieving higher quality education.

It is not my purpose here to explore the substantive issues of school finance reform but rather to contrast the dramatic rise in the states' assumption of local school expenditure with the proportionate share of state expenditures for local public libraries. In a study entitled *Improving State Aid to Public Libraries,* prepared by Government Studies and Systems for the Urban Libraries Council, the investigators comment upon the need for "a more equitable distribution of fiscal support among the three levels of government" [6, p. 2].[1] In 1975, they note, with data reported from forty-one states, that "local government provided 82 percent of public library expenditures, states provided 13 percent and the Federal government provided 5 percent" [ibid.]. These figures are then contrasted with the 1975 revenue pattern for the nation's public schools in which local government contributed 48.6 percent, the states 43.6 percent, and the federal government the remaining 7.8 percent. The national library averages do not, of course, reveal the wide disparity among various regions of the country. In the Rocky Mountain and far western areas of the United States the states' shares were 7 and 4 percent, respectively, whereas in the Southeast the states supplied 20 percent of total public library expenditures, and in the Middle Atlantic States, ranging from New York to Maryland, 18.7 percent.

There was also a considerable range in per capita expenditures. During 1975, New York State, using both state-aid funding and moneys appropriated to the state from the Library Services and Construction

---

1. In part, the data for this study draw upon another report prepared by the same corporate author [7]. It is important to note that some states were not able to complete the submitted questionnaires. Therefore, the footnotes accompanying the tables and the text in both of the studies should be noted with care.

Act (LSCA), made available $1.65 per capita, exclusive of local moneys, thus making New York the state with the highest per capita expenditure from state and federal revenues. Other states in the dollar-or-above category included Rhode Island, New Jersey, Maryland, Illinois, and Georgia. In terms of per capita expenditure, Colorado ranked lowest with $0.06 per capita, derived entirely from federal funds. It is interesting to note that, although states in the Southeast contributed 20 percent of the total library expenditures, Georgia was the only state in the region in the dollar-or-above range. With a state share of 36 percent and a federal share of 10 percent, Kentucky, for example, distributed $0.94 for local library development.

These figures and others cited in the Urban Libraries Council study raise several important issues. As of 1975, eleven states in the Union still had no program of state aid. The majority of those states having such programs contributed less than $1.00 per capita for local library service. The national average was $0.68, and the median was $0.53. The fiscal insignificance of these sums appears even more dramatic when they are compared with per capita expenditures derived from state aid for local public schools. In 1975 the national average was $146, the median $134.

I am not proposing here that public library expenditure from the state level should ever be comparable with state-level expenditure for the public schools in dollar amounts, but I am suggesting that the trend toward greater state assumption of local school financing is an important one which bears close scrutiny by the nation's public librarians. This is not merely a matter of raising more revenue but of reexamining our present modes of state-aid distribution.

Over one-half of state aid for schools is based on equalization formulas, and even further reduction in the disparity between the poorer and richer school districts is the primary rationale for the post-1971 trend in school finance reform. In contrast, as the Urban Libraries Council study notes, "only 7 percent of state aid (for libraries) is provided through equalization formulas" [6, p. 60], per capita distribution accounting for 45 percent of all state funds. Although this latter arrangement may prove administratively convenient, it is one little likely to reduce the difference between a poor library and its more affluent neighbor within the same state. Maryland, one of two states in the nation (the other is California) that base 100 percent of their state-aid programs on equalization formulas, is an outstanding example of what a state can accomplish through focusing aid in counties with relatively low property tax bases. New libraries and services in southern Maryland and along the eastern shore are witness to long-range planning by the state agency, which has used both state and federal funds to achieve this objective.

I realize that raising the level of state expenditures for local libraries may in some states prove difficult, if not impossible, especially in those states which have no income tax or those which can be characterized as largely rural and depopulated. At the same time, however, both historically and constitutionally, education has been considered a right, and concomitantly a responsibility, reserved to the states and to the people. Within recent years, the states have demonstrated that new or redirected revenues could be raised to equalize the fiscal base on which local education rests. The question begged here is whether or not the states can make the same effort for the public library. I do not possess a crystal ball and I cannot answer the question, but I devoutly hope that the relationship between the fiscal pattern for state support of local schools and that for public libraries would be a matter high on the agenda of the state conferences to be held in the coming months in anticipation of the 1979 White House Conference on Library and Information Services.

The Federal Government

In recent testimony before the Senate Subcommittee on Labor-HEW Appropriations, Eileen D. Cooke, the director of the American Library Association's Washington office, pointed to the bleak financial picture of public libraries, especially those in the major cities. ". . . Inflation," the testimony made clear, "continues to absorb dollars, whether in the cost of books (up 53 percent, to an $18.03 average, over the past five years), in magazine subscription prices (up 52 percent, to $24.59), which have risen far more rapidly than the overall inflation rate (up 36 percent since 1973), in wages and fringe benefits, or in the cost of energy needed to operate library buildings, most of which were not designed for energy efficiency. These costs are uncontrollable . . ." [8, p. 2]. Their effect on service may be gleaned from some of her examples: acquisitions cuts at the Free Library of Philadelphia, the closing of Sunday hours at the Denver Public Library, staff reductions and salary cuts at the Hartford Public Library in Connecticut, and the abandonment of sending out overdue notices at the Minneapolis Public Library.

It is inevitable at a time of straitened economy that the nation's librarians should look to the federal government for relief. Indeed, the library profession's first attempts to seek federal aid came during the period of the national depression of the 1930s. There is both logic and warranty to the librarians' position: the federal government is the nation's largest tax collector, and its revenues are derived from citizens not only of the country but also of Altoona and Paducah, Seattle and Cleveland, St. Louis and St. Paul. Why then, should not a greater proportion of federal funds be filtered back through the system to aid the readers and library users of these communities? I do not think that the federal government believes that libraries are unimportant; after all, members of Congress appropriate annually a rather sizable sum to support a library for themselves. The problem, as I have noted elsewhere, is one of priorities. Economist Alice M. Rivlin, now head of the Congressional Budget Office, puts the issue well: "The problem facing decision makers is the classic economic problem of allocating scarce resources among competing ends. What would do the most good? What do the analysts have to say about the *comparative* value of social action programs?" [9, p. 46].

There are no simple answers to these questions. The present administration faces the issue of declining urban areas, especially in the northeast corridor, and the severe economic problems of spiraling inflation and unemployment, highest among black youth. President Carter's proposed new urban policy program is modest: it will add only a few billion dollars to the $80 billion in federal aid which is already being directed to cities and states, and it places its primary emphasis on the private sector, offering loans and tax credits, among other inducements, to keep small businesses and corporations alive in urban areas. "Mr. Carter," recently commented a *New York Times* reporter, "brought to office a skepticism about Government's capacity to solve social problems and about the massive social spending of the 1960's" [10, p. 1].

In my book, *Federal Policy and Library Support* [11], I pointed to a number of the misgivings felt by the executive branch in its appraisal of federally supported library programs, namely, their institutional rather than client orientation and their lack of specific reflection of national goals, such as the social and economic improvement of poor people. In my view, these misgivings have not essentially changed. Originally conceived in the late 1930s as a social program to reach rural readers, an essentially unserved population group then representing one out of every three Americans, the Library Services and Construction Act (LSCA) now makes available, primarily on a per capita distribution formula, some $60 million annually for public library services and interlibrary cooperation.

Although some librarians expressed considerable optimism that a new administration, especially a Democratic one, would pump additional funds into the federal library legislation, others maintained a healthy skepticism. The luster of the New Frontier has gradually faded, the optimistic promise of the Great Society programs has not been fulfilled. Although President Carter's 1979 budget proposals did not "zero out" the library legislation, as did those of President Nixon in the 1974 budget, the LSCA requests for 1979 were modest: $56.9 million for Title I, public library services; no funds for Title II, construction; and only $3.337 million for Title III, interlibrary cooperation. The 1979 budget requests the exact amount appropriated in 1978. The nation's larger cities, those of 100,000 or more people, had hoped to benefit by the changes in the 1977 amended legislation, which earmarked for urban areas LSCA I funds above the $60 million floor that can be used for both urban and nonurban community libraries. Recently, the American Library Association presented its case to Congress, asking for a supplemental appropriation for 1978 and recommending for 1979 full funding of Title I ($140 million), Title II ($97 million), and Title III ($20 million), sums which represent the authorization levels stated in the legislation. If this additional funding is made available, California would stand to gain in 1979 an additional $8 million; New York, $7 million; Texas, $5 million; Illinois, Ohio, and Pennsylvania, more than $4 million. To reach the goals of the association, the federal program would have to be quadrupled, and in light of the present economy this does not seem likely.

Patterns of Support

Up to this point, this paper has summarized the current fiscal setting of the public library. The primary source of funding is realized through local taxes, chiefly the assessment on real estate. Such a tax has probably benefited suburban library growth since reassessment of suburban properties has increased revenue. Conversely, with the relocation of many businesses to suburban locations in avoidance of urban property taxes, the central-city libraries have not fared as well. The pattern of state support for local public libraries is highly varied. Since 1956, the year of the enactment of the Library Services Act, fifteen states have instituted programs of grants-in-aid, flat grants based upon geographic area, discretionary funds to aid local libraries, reimbursements, or other mechanisms. Thirty-eight states now have some means of subventing local service, leaving eleven states with no direct-aid programs, Hawaii, the twelfth state, being an exception because all public libraries are state supported.

At the federal level, the principle source of revenue has been the Library Services and Construction Act, although some public libraries have received moneys from revenue sharing and specific legislative enactments for Model Cities, the arts and the humanities, and other priorities of interest to the national government. This latter revenue, however, is sporadic and, in some cases, discretionary in nature, being linked to a particular project with a definite termination date.

The legislative history of LSCA has been checkered. The last year for which the administration actually requested the full authorization figure for Title I was 1966. Since that time the administration has in general followed the pattern of requesting for the next fiscal year the amounts

expended for the program during the previous year or, as in the case of
the Nixon administration, no money at all. Congress has been more
generous in raising recent administration requests, although the full
authorization for LSCA, Title I, has not been realized since 1967. In
assembling the data for their study of state aid to libraries, Government
Studies and Systems found that, with forty states reporting, total
expenditures for public libraries, that is, from all levels of government,
exceeded the billion-dollar mark for the time in 1975, a year in which, on
a national basis, the per capita expenditure was $5.83 [6, p. 19].

From the depression period until the present, students of public
library revenues have attempted some formulation of the proper balance among local, state, and national funds. Carleton Joeckel was one of
the first students of library finance to address this issue, which he did in
his landmark report for President Roosevelt's Advisory Commission on
Education, *Library Service* [12]. Later, Lowell Martin was to recommend a
pattern of 50 percent local, 30 percent state, and 20 percent federal.
Recently Rodney Lane and his associates, the authors of the Urban
Libraries Council study, have suggested 30 percent local, 50 percent
state, and 20 percent federal [13, p. 69]. Certainly, the whole area of
intergovernmental relations or fiscal federalism is an important one, and
I do not wish to denigrate it here. But the financial setting of the public
library includes not only the matter of revenue sources but also the
question of expenditure. Where is the money going? Who is benefitting
from it? What does the public get from the public library?

The Problem of Priorities of Service

Addressing an assemblage very similar to this in 1967, on the occasion of
the thirty-second conference of the Graduate Library School, Harold S.
Hacker said: "The solution to our financial problems depends upon our
ability to persuade the leaders of our local, state, and national governments of the necessity of our services to the public and of our critical
need for more funds" [14, p. 57]. Hacker concluded his address with this
comment: "I am afraid that our record to date, while promising, has not
been very productive" [ibid.]. Ten years later, I can only come to the
same conclusion. My assessment is based in part on my perception that
the public library, in all too many communities, is not addressing itself to
the political and social realities of the times. Nor do I think for one
minute that the present crisis of the public library can be solely cured
through a massive infusion of funds.

It is a sobering thought that within the next quarter of a century
American librarianship is going to face the burden of transferring the
cultural content in terms of publications and holdings of the twentieth

century into the twenty-first. This feat has never really been handled in this country: public libraries are a mid-nineteenth-century phenomenon, and academic libraries, although older, did not begin their massive acquisitions programs until the conferring of the doctorate became accepted in academe, and that date is generally regarded as 1876, the year marking the foundation of the Johns Hopkins University. Of course, there have been retrospective acquisitions, but for the most part the contents of libraries in this country really date only to the mid-nineteenth century.

Founded as an agency which would disseminate utilitarian and recreational reading matter for the general populace, the public library in all too many inner-city communities now finds itself encrusted with an older collection of interest primarily to antiquarians and scholars. At the same time, faced with rising personnel costs, many of these same libraries are putting proportionately less and less of their budgets into the purchase of multiple copies of new and popular books.

The Enoch Pratt Free Library in Baltimore could be taken as a case in point. In 1886, James Hodges, then mayor of Baltimore, compared the functions of the learned library established in the city by George Peabody with the anticipated role of the one founded by Enoch Pratt. "The Peabody Library is a grand foundation," he wrote, "worthy of the generous man to whom it owes its existence, and its stores are of inestimable value; but it is of a different character, and meets other wants. Mr. Pratt's design was to found a library of good reading, for the entire public, of books which might be read at the fireside, and should carry their stores of knowledge, of beauty, or of innocent recreation, to the homes of the people" [15, pp. 65–66].

It seems to me that the mayor's comments contained little augury that the Enoch Pratt Free Library was ever intended to serve as a research center, yet in some ways that is what the Enoch Pratt Free Library over the course of the years has become. Its situation is in no way so very different from that of Cleveland, Chicago, Philadelphia, Detroit, Minneapolis, Denver, or St. Louis. More and more the attention of these libraries is being directed toward their role as statewide backups for local libraries which lie outside their jurisdiction, yet within their own jurisdictions the dissemination functions of these libraries in terms of circulation registers little growth or is declining. Is not the real need one of looking at priorities?

In Hacker's essay, to which I have made reference, several recommendations were made to increase revenue sources for the large public library. The first was participation in a regional mode as a backstop for smaller units of service. The second was the expansion of revenues through possible merger with surrounding counties or else contracts with them for additional services. Next came increased state and federal aid, with mention of the possibility of charging for certain specialized services. And finally, the suggestion was made that improved management and mechanization might aid in the resolution of fiscal problems [14, pp. 53–57].

In actuality, many of the solutions mentioned by Hacker have been implemented. Increasingly, the states have recognized the major urban libraries as resource centers. Contracts have been arranged between suburban and urban libraries. Since 1967, when Hacker wrote, both state and federal aid has increased. The possibility of charging fees has become, in recent months, a national issue, and a committee has been appointed by the American Library Association to design a research proposal to examine more closely the implications of fee-based services in a free public library. And certainly, if the attention paid to such matters in the library press is any barometer, public libraries are adopting changed catalog formats, such as computer output microfiche and computerized circulation systems.

All of this activity, however, raises a fundamental question: Are public libraries doing all of these things to increase the revenue or to augment and improve the service? Last year the Maryland interlibrary loan network handled over 67,000 referrals. Important as these requests may have been, their numbers are miniscule when compared with the 24,350,191 items circulated to the general public by that state's public libraries, exclusive of the circulation in Baltimore City. While the backstopping function is important, it does not displace the primary responsibility of the public library for neighborhood and community-level service, an area in which many inner-city public libraries are proving weakest.

The Problem of the Central Library

In a study of Oakland, California, published in 1974, three policy planners from the University of California, Berkeley, devoted particular attention to the situation of its public library system during the late 1960s and early 1970s. In 1965–66, Oakland spent 79 percent of its budget on salaries and 6 percent on library materials. Although the central library was responsible for only 25 percent of the circulation, it received 60 percent of all expenditures for personnel and acquisitions. Funds were allocated to the branches on the basis of proved circulation, and all titles purchased conformed to standards established by the main library [16, p. 223]. In summary, the researchers commented: "The combination of poor and often irrelevant collections, a small total branch budget, the vicious circulation-allocation cycle, and the consequent deterioration of poverty-area buildings means that the branch system provides little education or recreation for those city residents who need it most" [16, p. 200].

In their analysis of the central library, the investigators raised questions as to the utility of some of its collections: "Oakland can be justly proud of the California Room, with its fine collection concerning California history dating from the 1850s. . . . Nevertheless, one might ask if it would not be more appropriate for the University of California, possibly the Bancroft Library, to take over the historical collection. Since the collection really serves the state rather than the city, perhaps there should be state sharing of the cost of maintaining it. In view of its exceedingly low usage by city residents it is difficult to justify the cost of the collection" [16, p. 213]. The investigators also questioned the expense inherent in the high-level reference functions performed by the central library, making the point that user charges could be assessed for business and industrial clients.

The Oakland example does not prove the rule, but the difficulties of funding allocations in library systems with central libraries is worth contrasting with suburban or county systems which do not have these retrospective collections. In a compilation of data prepared by the Montgomery County (Md.) Public Library, which ranked the performance of thirty urban and suburban public libraries serving large population areas in 1977, Baltimore County, Maryland, is shown to rank first in per capita library material support, first in per capita circulation, first in workload per staff member, and third in per capita support. Baltimore County maintains no central library. By contrast the Baltimore city library ranked tenth in per capita material support, twenty-fourth in per capita circulation, twenty-eighth in workload per staff member, and fifth in total per capita support. Of the thirty libraries examined, the Detroit Public Library, again one with a large central library, ranked lowest in per capita library material support, lowest in per capita circulation, twenty-ninth in the workload per staff member, and nineteenth in per capita support [17].

These are, of course, gross measurements, but they do demonstrate that the older industrial cities with their downtown main libraries are putting the largest expenditure of their funds into salaries at the expense of acquisitions. The newer systems, on the other hand, having fewer personnel are allocating a higher proportion of funds for the purchase of materials and sustain a higher circulation rate per capita. There are, of course, many other factors which must be taken into account, such as that of municipal overburden, which some economists believe renders costs for the same services higher in the cities than in the nonurban areas, and a whole host of complicated socioeconomic issues, such as personal income, years of completed schooling, and level of literacy, all of which render sharp contrasts between urban and nonurban residents.

Today, all too often, public libraries in the central cities are caught in a bind, maintaining massive retrospective collections whose use by suburban and exurban residents will probably never be very extensive while at the same time reducing resources and services to their own client groups. Dismantling these collections, as mentioned in the Oakland study, is an extreme remedy, and in light of local pride, local trustees, and local governance probably will not take place. Aside from dismantling, however, there needs to be some examination of matters affecting future growth. To attempt to purchase definitively in fields of contemporary knowledge for the use of present and future generations is a legitimate objective for the research institutions, but I do not think it should be the primary goal of the public library. In the present fiscal crisis affecting all libraries in this country, the academic libraries are facing up more realistically to the fiscal crunch than their sister public institutions. Dead storage for little used materials, defining shared responsibilities for collection building with other research libraries within a given geographic area, and a greater concern for a more systematic analysis of work flow to reduce cost are all matters that have been seriously addressed by the larger academic libraries. An example of these concerns is furnished by the Conference on No-Growth Budgets, held in 1976 at Indiana State University, the proceedings of which make interesting reading [18].

The nation's public libraries cannot be, nor were they ever, all things to all people. Too great a concern for building a statewide network may be obscuring the fact that reading and library usage continue to accelerate in the nation's middle-income suburbs and to decline in low-income areas of the central city. I believe that reversing that decline would be possible if less attention and support were given to the main library and branch library circulation were to become the number one priority of the urban public library. Having both a great central repository and also an effective distributive system may be highly desirable, but if a choice must be made between them I would have to opt for the latter rather than the former. It is becoming fashionable today to claim that the public library has never had much effect on the poor, yet I can point to the writings of I. I. Rabi, Ralph Ellison, Kenneth Clark, James Baldwin, Mary Antin, Theodore Dreiser, Karl Shapiro, and many others to show the effect of public library usage on these distinguished Americans when they were young. Poor the majority of them were in terms of income, but they were most certainly not poor in spirit, or intelligence, or talent. As children they read their way through the holdings of children's reading rooms, mostly in branch libraries, and made the discoveries by which each new generation re-creates from past artifacts new forms of art and culture.

The Future of Public Library Financing

I said at the beginning of this paper that the public library could not be regarded as an integer. It operates within a society which, as Daniel Bell pointed out in his book, *The Cultural Contradictions of Capitalism*, is no longer of itself integral, but in Bell's phrase, "disjunctive," governed by different, even contrary, axial principles, and responding to different norms, and different rhythms of change [19, p. 10]. "The fundamental political fact," wrote Bell,

"in the second half of the twentieth century has been the extension of *state-directed economies*. These developed first because of the need to rescue the system from depression, later because of the demands of a war economy and the enlargement of military commitments, and finally because of the strategic role of fiscal policy in affecting levels of spending and patterns of investment. In the last quarter of the twentieth century, we now move to *state-managed societies*. And these emerge because of the increase in the large-scale social demands (health, education, welfare, social services) which have become entitlements for the population. The new "class struggles" of the post-industrial society are less a matter of conflict between management and worker in the economic enterprise than the pull and tug of various organized segments to influence the state budget. Where state expenditure approximates 40 percent of Gross National Product, as it almost does in the United States . . . the chief political issues become the allocation of monies and the incidence of taxation." [19, pp. 24–25]

I introduce Bell's comments here because I believe they state the case quite clearly that the future financial setting of the public library will be increasingly politicized. Over 100 years ago Americans began to accept the provision of reading matter from a locally tax-supported agency. Their pursuit of self-education was entirely voluntary and directed by such of their personal interests as curiosity, aesthetic appreciation, or a need for recreation. Today, the pursuit of reading is spoken of as a "right," as in the "right-to-read" movement. The extension of educational opportunity, even to the provision of publicly supported higher education, has become an entitlement. During the past century, the public library has developed new competitors for its share of the educational tax dollar: community colleges, museums, educational parks, preschooling programs, continuing education—all now make a claim upon the public purse. How well the public library will survive in this competition depends largely on the political skills of the librarians themselves. Building a constituency is an important factor in attracting support—that is one reason why I rate the extension and distributive system of the public library so highly.

The other reason, and the far more important one, is that although research institutions are and will continue to be responsive to the needs of future scholarship, the population of our inner cities and our expanding suburbs have needs for reading and information that are not necessarily related to scholarship. The rise of suburban library usage, when compared with the decline in the larger and older cities, only points to the growing divisiveness in our society, in which the poor grow poorer and the rich get richer. It is the essential dilemma inherent in the current plight of the public library that networking, which seems to hold out promise for new revenue support from government, will tend, however unintentional that process may be, to exacerbate the distinctions between the haves and have-nots of this country. Committed library users will tend to make use of the network for further enrichment; conversely, it will remain valueless to nonusers of local nodes of service, such as public libraries. The public library cannot be expected to redress the economic balance of power in the United States, but it can and should add its measure of utility to the enhancement of individual lives. The price being paid to support an ever-growing subject departmentalized main library may simply be too high in this economy. On the agenda for future public librarians must be a reexamination of the purpose of the public library—provision of books and materials "to the homes of the people." Facing an uncertain period in the economy, the nation's public libraries need to rethink the output side of their ledgers. The future of today's most gifted children, many of them leaders of tomorrow, lies in that balance sheet. Such children have, shall I dare say it, a "right" of access to an unmortgaged public library.

REFERENCES

1. Vitz, Carl, ed. *Current Problems in Public Library Finance*. Chicago: American Library Association, 1933.
2. Duffus, R. L. *Our Starving Libraries*. Boston: Houghton Mifflin Co., 1933.
3. Hughes, Langston. *The Big Sea: An Autobiography*. New York: Alfred A. Knopf, Inc., 1940.
4. Rosen, Sumner M., ed. *Economic Power Failure: The Current American Crisis*. New York: McGraw-Hill Book Co., 1975.
5. Fiske, Edward B. "Tax Reform: Does It Balance Rich and Poor?" *New York Times* (November 13, 1977), sec. 12.
6. Government Studies and Systems, Inc. *Improving State Aid to Public Libraries*. Washington, D.C.: National Commission on Libraries and Information Science, 1977.
7. Government Studies and Systems, Inc. *Evaluation of the Effectiveness of Federal Funding of Public Libraries*. Washington, D.C.: National Commission on Libraries and Information Science, 1976.

8. Cooke, Eileen D. "Statement . . . before the Senate Subcommittee on Labor-HEW Appropriations on FY 1979 Labor-HEW Appropriations Bill, March 16, 1978." Unpublished typescript.

9. Rivlin, Alice M. *Systematic Thinking for Social Action*. Washington, D.C.: Brookings Institution, 1971.

10. Reinhold, Robert. "How Urban Policy Gets Made—Very Carefully." *New York Times* (April 2, 1978), sec. 4.

11. Molz, Redmond Kathleen. *Federal Policy and Library Support*. Cambridge, Mass.: M.I.T. Press, 1976.

12. Joeckel, Carleton. *Library Service*. Washington, D.C.: Government Printing Office, 1938.

13. Government Studies and Systems, Inc. *Alternatives for Financing the Public Library*. Washington, D.C.: Government Printing Office, 1974.

14. Hacker, Harold S. "Financial Problems of the Large Library." In *The Public Library in the Urban Setting*, edited by Leon Carnovsky. Chicago: University of Chicago Press, 1968.

15. Hodges, James. "Address of Hon. James Hodges, Mayor." In *Enoch Pratt Free Library: Letters and Documents Relating to Its Foundation and Organization*. Baltimore: Isaac Friendenwald, 1886.

16. Levy, Frank; Meltsner, Arnold J.; and Wildavsky, Aaron. *Urban Outcomes: Schools, Streets, and Libraries*. Berkeley: University of California Press, 1974.

17. Green, Joseph. "Urban and Suburban Public Library Statistics." Chart VI. Montgomery County Department of Public Libraries, 1978. Unpublished.

18. Lee, Sul H., ed. *Library Budgeting: Critical Challenges for the Future*. Ann Arbor, Mich.: Pierian Press, 1977.

19. Bell, Daniel. *The Cultural Contradictions of Capitalism*. New York: Basic Books, 1976.

THE TECHNOLOGICAL SETTING OF THE PUBLIC LIBRARY

Kenneth E. Dowlin

There are four major categories of resources that public libraries must use in order to be viable public service institutions: (1) the capabilities of the thousands of people who work in them; (2) the printed and audiovisual materials that the members of their communities need to fill their time and enrich their lives; (3) the facilities in which the materials and staff are housed and which provide a readily identifiable location for the interaction of users, staff, and materials; and (4) technology. In most public libraries, this last resource is overlooked as such; it is on this resource that I want to concentrate in this paper.

It can be argued that the publishing industry has lessened the dependence of the public on libraries for printed materials. Even though our society is reading more, it is relying less on the public library as a source of reading material [1, pp. 6, 34]. The impact of paperbacks and mass periodicals, as well as the existence of book clubs and a multitude of book stores, has diminished the general public's need for popular books or mass-circulation books to be supplied by public libraries. The growth of the community college and the dramatic expansion of higher education has lessened the need for the library to supply the kinds of educational materials which allowed it to function as the "poor man's university."

The Information-Utility Concept

If the need for public libraries to provide materials in these areas has lessened, has the role of the library in the community diminished? I think not. Our citizens must still have access to a wide range of information and materials not readily available through the channels mentioned above. And while there are abundant sources of information for the community, access to them is complex and often little understood [2, p. 20].

Just as the library has in the past served as the community focal point for access to books, it should now serve as the focal point for access to information. Moreover, the library should become a community resource not only for the general public's information but for other agencies as well. It is clear that information access will become crucial to our society, and it has been suggested that mass-information utilities will become major change agents in our society [3, abstract]. The impact of rapid social change on the library will be to change its role in the community, but in order to perform its new role the library will have to refocus its efforts [4, abstract]. I would emphasize that the public library has the potential to become an important community information utility and urge that we focus our efforts to this end.

While the library is not unique in the community in the use of technology for the provision of information, it could become so if it would bring information technology together with its long history of public service, publicly owned facilities and materials, and a neutral stance on the use of the information. It could achieve a dimension of service not available in any other community agency.

The public library can continue to supply the traditional sources of information when appropriate. In addition, however, it can serve as the local link to the regional and national networks that are developing with the aid of the new technologies. The attention of libraries was focused initially on developing networks in relation to cataloging functions. We have moved to the use of networks for computerized bibliographical searches. A logical progression is to go to computerized information networking. What is missing is acceptance of the enlarged concept of information services and the ability to use the new information technology locally.

My view is that the primary function of the public library of the future will be in the informational services that it provides [5, p. 108]. I argue that the potential impact of technology is as great, and in the future may be greater, than that of any of the other resources available to the public library as it becomes a community information utility.

The Nature of the Technology

First we must rid ourselves of the notion that technology applies only to factories or assembly lines [6, p. 25]. We must understand technology's ability to change society and alter the way that man thinks and how he perceives his world [6, p. 29]. We are undergoing the same type of evolutionary experience that civilization underwent when the printing press was introduced [7, p. viii]. At present we are less interested in using the new technology for new purposes than we are in cataloging, indexing, and providing access to existing materials.

There are three modern, major technological resources that the library needs to use. They are as follows:

1. Microforms. Microforms can provide mass storage for data bases

locally produced and rapid access to the material filmed, and can serve as a cost-effective alternate to computer storage. Several companies provide microform-based information-storage systems which interface with a computer for access.

2. Video and other audiovisual media. These can be used to capture local events, to expand the role of the library for programming and presentations, and to involve new segments of the community with the library.

3. The computer. The computer can provide instant access to important data, link the library with other data bases, maintain the inventory of all of a library's materials, and provide a means for efficient housekeeping and management.

In addition, there are other technologies of which we must be aware. Facsimile transmission has been around for over fifty years. Today's equipment is vastly superior to that of just a few years ago [8, pp. 10–11, 37]. The Minnesota Mining and Manufacturing Company (3M) has a facsimile transceiver that operates as a normal photocopier when not used for transmission or receipt of documents [9, unpaged]. Several libraries communicate with deaf users via TWX (teletypewriter exchange) machines. Color photocopiers, slow-scan video, and citizens band radio should be explored for their ability to increase the library's potential to serve.

The computer has had the most impact on library operations of any current technologies. A DIALOG Search of the ERIC file[1] on the term, "computer and libraries," provided 1,274 citations, while a search on "video and libraries" provided only 607 citations. The use of microfilm production equipment for the creation of local data bases is evidenced by only thirty-one citations.

Extent of Use of Computers

It is projected that the in-house minicomputer will be the major thrust of development for technology in libraries in the 1980s [10, abstract]. But how widespread is the use of the computer systems in public libraries? One recent publication, *Library Automation: The State of the Art II* [11], gives no references to computerized systems in public libraries or any indication that public libraries have contributed to the state of automation in libraries. Nevertheless, the book does indicate the range of functions performed by computers in libraries, and some or all of them are currently being carried out in public libraries. A number of public

1. This was a search using Lockheed's DIALOG service, which provides on-line access to a large number of machine-readable bibliographic data bases.

libraries, for example, are using computer-generated book catalogs, computer-output microfilm catalogs, and automated circulation systems, or have access to Ohio College Library Center (OCLC) or other data bases. From this handbook, it is clear that there are no libraries that do all of the functions on the same machine. This is equally true of public libraries, and I contend that the major issue for computers in the 1980s will be achieving a synthesis of computerized systems. It took computers a decade to be able to communicate with each other. It still requires a conscious design to provide telecommunication links between computers' central processing units. There are many libraries now operating multiple systems that do not communicate with any of their other systems. The increased interest in turnkey systems[2] will aggravate the situation.

The lack of impact of computer technology on public libraries is further suggested by the general lack of awareness of people in technological fields about public libraries. In most books on information technology I find no references to public libraries and few references to any libraries. In reading those books I see many topics that could be related to the library, but none of the authors seems to consider the library as a factor in providing information to society.

Information Technology and Library Support

Let us be blunt about one of the values of developing the use of the new information technology in the public library. The solidity and extent of the financial base of any library is directly related to the leverage that the library has over its funding sources. These sources may be city, county, state, or federal government. Most of the libraries that have excellent financial support have slowly developed a historic base for this in their communities. Libraries that lack this historic base of firm support must find ways of developing it, and given the changing nature of our society this is increasingly difficult.

The presence of information specialists on a library's staff and the technology to provide rapid information systems can help the library gain support in the circles that fund the library. The library in Natrona County, Wyoming, for example, has had excellent success in increasing its budget. Part of the reason was that the library designed, implemented, and operated the county-records information system used by the county officials. It can be argued that though these officials still do not understand the importance of the traditional functions of the

2. "Turnkey" systems are preprogrammed package systems available commercially and designed for specific tasks.

library, they did realize that the economic well being of the library directly affected the operation of their information system. After the Natrona County Public Library initiated the county-records system, the presentation of the library's annual budget became a much more rewarding experience.

The Pikes Peak Library is for the first time moving into a service that is actively desired by the funding bodies of the area. It has received a federal contract to implement a community car-pooling program. The library received this contract because (1) it had the computer that could do the task, and (2) its staff could write the project request to obtain the funds. Another program, the Citizens Action Line Limited, was located in the library because it had the computer, the space, and had expressed its commitment to the community information center concept. This program uses Junior League volunteers to man telephones to locate agencies to solve citizens' problems and to follow up the contacts on a regular basis.

Here we see exhibited one of the valid uses of technology in the library: as a means of building a dependence on the library by the agencies in the community. It is much more difficult to deny the library's requests for funding all its services if the city depends on the library for one or more services that are integral to the city's operation. Traditional public library service does not in itself usually build this strong dependence, yet public libraries need such commitment of support if they are to create top-notch library services in their community. Moreover, there are no strong external pressures to influence this kind of support. We do not have accreditation agencies or the American Bar Association to implement standards or enforce norms.

Costs of Technology

There are other practical matters that should influence the development of computer technology in the public library. Few library administrators are aware of the dramatic cost effectiveness of minicomputers and microcomputers. It is possible to project an annual personnel-cost increase of 10 percent per year from now on. It is also possible to argue that the use of technology to its fullest can offset this increase. The library administrator's excuse for not using computers because of their expense is no longer acceptable because costs have been decreasing.

Let us look at the downward movement of computer costs. The cost for an 8080 central processing unit (cpu) is $6,750. The 8080 is an industry standard for micros and is roughly comparable to the IBM Model 30 in terms of data-path widths, number of registers, instruction execution time, and maximum memory size [12, p. 213]. If my memory serves me, the rent on the system when I learned to program it in 1968 was in the vicinity of $50 per wall clock hour. The monthly lease would have been in the neighborhood of $8,000–$10,000 per month. The cost to the Pikes Peak Regional Library for its in-house PDP 11/70 is 17¢ per cpu minute as compared to $3.00 per cpu minute on the El Paso County DEC 10 that the library used to start its systems development three years ago. The 11/70 is one-sixth the cost of the 10 that it replaced. The replacement for the 11/70 may have the same cost differential.

But library administrators say that the programming is too expensive. The major cost of program development is related to systems analysis, file structures, and data relationships. The library staff should have the skills for the systems analysis and for determining the data relationships, and the state libraries or networks should be providing assistance in these areas. If we could get over our syndrome of every library for itself we could overcome present difficulties.

The file structures, on the other hand, can be provided by hardware or vendor's software. General Electric, for example, markets an associative processor that manages files, retrieves and stores data, and allows access to any word or combination of characters that is requested. It string searches any file at a rate of 400,000 characters per second. Searchers make up their data relationships as they design the search. It is not necessary to develop the file structures before the data are entered. The associative processor allows a combination of characters or data strings up to 256 characters in any configuration that is wanted. In a cataloger's terms this would allow access to any word in the main entry card and use of any combinations of words in that record in order to retrieve any record. It also allows the retrieval of only the information desired. If only the titles of a particular author are wanted, the screen displays only the titles.[3] It is possible to configure a data system using the associative processor, a PDP 11/05 cpu, a 200 megabyte disk drive, and miscellaneous equipment for a purchase price of $90,000. If this cost is amortized over seven years and an intelligent college student is hired to operate the system, it is possible to have a general purpose computer in-house for less than $26,360 per year. This is less than the cost of four employees now, and in five years that will have dropped to nearly two. The hardware cost will remain fixed over the seven years.

Other configurations are possible. A look at the magazine *Datamation* shows a General Automation 440 Data Series computer priced below $45,000 which includes COBOL for programming, support for fifteen terminals, and 128 kbyte main memory [13, pp. 34–35]. This system would handle circulation, inventory, ordering, and housekeeping tasks

---

3. Telephone conversation with Vera Vaswani, General Electric Space Division, Arlington, Virginia, January 6, 1978.

in a library serving 100,000 people. How about a computer system for under $3,000? I can configure one for $2,677. It includes a central processor, a cathode ray tube terminal (CRT), a printer, floppy disk storage (a form of high-density data storage on disks), and communications interface. This computer would provide a circulation system in a small library. IASIS makes a "computer-in-a-book" for $495 [14].

But the library administrator says that the peripherals are too expensive. A Hazeltine 1500 cathode ray tube terminal now costs $998. We are using them for all new terminal acquisitions instead of the Hazeltine 2000s that we purchased two years ago for $1,600. We are reselling the 2000s for $75 less than we paid for them two years ago! Houston Instruments provides a 100-character-per-second printer for $795. The development of "bubble" memory portends a great future for economical data storage. Texas Instruments sells this in their terminals at $500 for 20,000 bytes. Storage costs for semiconductor memory have decreased nearly two-thirds in three years [13, p. 150].

Developmental Trends

It is extremely important for the system designers of today to be aware of future trends in data processing. The rapid rate of change in computer technology is making a two- or three-year development program for computer systems unfeasible. Unless the system provides partial benefits immediately and retains flexibility, it will not be cost effective. Many long-range programs are outmoded before they are completed. I would estimate that the time required to develop a BAL-LOTS[4] or OCLC system today might be less than half the original time.

The trend in data processing today is toward distributive processing. A distributive-processing system allows the nodes of a system to process their systems work locally but ties them to a network which links them with other nodes and with the central headquarters. One of the country's largest banks, for example, has replaced its large centralized data-processing center with a network of minicomputers located in each facility. The major library networks, however, show little inclination to foster distributed processing. Nevertheless, the development of distributive processing will become necessary as libraries are forced to develop a balance between centralization and decentralization of data bases. It is not economically feasible to centralize all of the necessary automation for all of the libraries in a state or region, for the costs of communications have not shown as dramatic a decline as the cost of computer hardware.

4. BALLOTS (Bibliographic Automation of Large Library Operations Using Time Sharing) is a system developed by Stanford University.

In our own case, for example, it is cheaper for a user of the Colorado Career Information System to pay for a duplicate system in Colorado Springs than it is to pay communications costs to Denver, only seventy miles away. Until we develop, through distributive processing, the ability to implement our own systems and to tie these systems into the resources available through networks, libraries will be tied to the systems developed by OCLC, BALLOTS, CLSI and other agencies. It is important to gain the flexibility possible through mixed processing. I do not believe that all communities, and thus all libraries, are alike. Each library needs to develop its strengths, and these strengths should be based on its own community. Our efforts to create networks should not provide homogenized libraries. Mixed processing places a major burden on the local library which must have the capability of using the resources of the network in an effective way but has to go beyond the capabilities of the network as required by its own particular needs and circumstances.

In 1975 I made the statement that critical mass was crucial to the development of sophisticated automated systems [5, p. 110]. This still holds true. What has changed is that the state of technology has dramatically reduced the mass required. I believed then that it would require a library with an annual circulation of over 1 million volumes to consider computerization seriously. I would now reduce that to 150,000, and within five years that figure will be less than 100,000. The general purpose minicomputer is important here because it facilitates the use of several functional systems on the same central processor. Multiple use of hardware allows a piece of equipment that is too expensive for one function to become cost effective. Our terminals, for example, allow use of DIALOG, BALLOTS, ORBIT, INFOBANK,[5] the county computer, and the in-house computer. This is achieved by purchasing terminals that meet the national standards for data communications. All components of the hardware for a circulation system are now available in individual pieces. In 1975 when I first started to develop our circulation system none of the companies supplying circulation systems would supply individual components. These are now available off the shelf. Thus the user can now custom design his configuration. Very few library administrators would accept a prefabricated main building, a preselected collection, or staff hired by a vendor, yet they show little inclination to question the compatibility of turnkey packages in automation.

It is ironic that the ideal public library, in terms of community services, tends to be the small library. The staff can know the complete collection,

5. ORBIT is the name of the System Development Corporation's (SDC) data-base service. INFOBANK is the name of the *New York Times* data bank which contains indexing not only for that newspaper but for a number of other newspapers and journals as well.

the patrons, and the nonusers in their community. They can use this
knowledge to provide more effective use of resources to solve the
informational problems of their communities. Unfortunately, they often
lack the resources to provide the assistance needed by the community.
The use of computers and access to networks and regional service
systems can help the small library obtain these resources. Larger
libraries, because of size and complexity, frequently cannot manage their
resources in a timely way to bring them to bear on the problems that
users bring to the library. The computer has the potential to allow the
large library to operate in a mode similar to that of the small library. If
the larger library has a general purpose computer that is on-line to all its
facilities and has the knowledge to use that computer, it can provide
some of the intimate, patron-oriented services that the small library
provides to its users. The computer can be used not only for materials-
inventory purposes but for an inventory of community resources and
the human resources of the library, communication between the library's
units, training, supplying access to unpublished materials, information
on user needs and interests, facilities and equipment inventory, and
information on the use of these resources by the community. It can
release staff time from clerical tasks so that this time can be used to assist
the user or to reach the nonuser, as well as to increase the library's ability
to do a variety of housekeeping chores.

Pikes Peak Regional Library

In order to assure you that these systems are feasible, let me discuss the
developments at the Pikes Peak Regional Library. The library has been
developing on-line systems since August 1975, and a current list of
operational systems includes:

1. The circulation system that charges materials out, charges them in,
provides patron validation plus renewals and overdues, maintains the
reserve list, locates and identifies the status of the books, and provides
current statistics that allow the supervisor to evaluate the degree of
proficiency of the system's operators.

2. A personnel directory maintained on-line by my secretary that
includes the current addresses and telephone numbers of all employees.
A current printed directory can be produced on demand.

3. A personnel log that includes the dates for raises and evaluations of
all employees and their current classifications, departments, and divisions. This file can produce lists of employees by class, department, or
even birthdays.

4. A community events calendar which includes all activities in the

community available to the public. This system can produce a current list on demand by the terminal operator.

5. The budget system which allows allocation of funds, the massaging of the budget during preparation, and the production and distribution of copies of the current draft and any revisions to it. This allows the budget to be an effective planning document.

6. The accounting system which allows immediate posting of checks, produces the check register, and provides monthly reports to all supervisors. This report shows expenditures, the budget figure, and the current balance and indicates the spending level apportioned over twelve months. Any modifications in the budget during the year are immediately reflected in the monthly reports.

7. The management-information system which collects data and totals it according to categories and programs provided in the budget. The programs also correspond to the accounting subdivisions. At present the statistics are fed into the system by the department heads who must validate any figures used. At some future point some of the statistics will be collected directly from other computer programs.

8. A system that allows communications between the terminals. The systems officer, for example, transmits memos to my terminal which are then printed. He retains a file of these memos on-line.

9. An ordering system which maintains the order files, prints the orders, calculates the balance of funds on a demand basis, and provides statistics of orders sent, books received, and the running discount.

10. A periodicals-inventory system which is done with the computer's text editor. It is not the most sophisticated system in the world, but it works.

11. The library presently has access to BALLOTS, ORBIT, DIALOG, and INFOBANK systems, and the county computer as well as the in-house PDP-11 computer.

12. The library is the local supplier for the Colorado Career Information System for school districts, state and local manpower agencies, and its own users.

The library has commitments to develop additional systems—some of which have been mentioned earlier—during this year:

1. A human resources file to be used by the library's staff, the volunteers of the CALL (Citizens' Action Line, Ltd.) project, and the community.

2. A car-pool information center funded by the federal Department of Transportation.

3. The library has a contract for the Instant Response Ordering System from Bro-Dart. This system will be on-line to Bro-Dart's Pennsylvania warehouse and will allow the library to check the inventory before ordering.

4. Since the library handles its own funds, a cash flow–analysis system is under development.

The library considers on-line systems development as an operating function for the library for as far as our planning extends. Systems that are in the planning stages of development are:

1. Complete automation of all processing functions other than physical preparation of materials. Our goal is to reduce the present processing cost per title from $4.62 to $2.00 and to provide an average throughput time of forty-eight hours. The Instant Response Ordering System will be accessed through the in-house computer, thereby allowing access to the system by all terminals and the use of record spin-offs for processing.

2. Local manipulation of data from network sources to provide support for data bases and systems used in the operation of the library. An example will be to use BALLOTS to create catalog cards.

3. A learning-resources file which will support the educational brokering services of the library and the consortium for continuing education in the Pikes Peak Region.

4. An on-line interlibrary-loan system which searches the inventory of the library and the locator file of other libraries in the system, prints all forms, and collects statistics. Our goal is to reduce the present cost of $4.00 and time of twenty minutes per transaction by 50 percent.

5. An on-line public catalog for 1981. The system for this will require modeling at least five different designs before implementation can begin.

6. An on-line policy and procedures manual which will be accessible by CRT to all units of the library. This will allow instant update of the manual, access by keywords, and immediate printing.

As time allows, the library would also like to investigate:

1. Computer-assisted instruction in the use of the library for the patron.

2. Computer-assisted instruction for the staff.

3. An on-line program for introducing children to the concept of information services. We are planning to include information of specific interest to children in the library's information data base.

4. A terminal at the checkout counter to tally the patrons' satisfaction with services provided. It will operate in an interactive mode and will ask specific questions.

5. A system to allow community agencies to use a dial-up terminal to read files on community resources.

6. Specialized accounting components to allocate costs and anticipate future needs for equipment and supplies.

7. An on-line furniture and equipment inventory.

8. The interfacing of local data bases and data bases accessible through the networks into the local cable television system. This has been

explored with the cable television operator, but they are unwilling to commit the start-up costs.

The management information and accounting systems we have set up or are setting up are extremely important to the development process. Taken in conjunction, they provide information on the cost of current and future systems. The traditional methodology of cost studies can no longer keep up with technological developments. They have become tools for a semistatic institution.

Returning to the statement with which I began the paper, I would like to repeat that it is now technically possible and economically feasible for the library to become the community information utility by using computer technology.

Microfilm

The other technologies, however, also have their part. They must also be considered as tools for increasing the effectiveness and flexibility of the community information utility. Based on my DIALOG search, it appears that few public libraries are using microfilm in a production sense. While designing the county-records system for the county offices in Casper, I grew to realize the potential of microfilm in a public library. Microfilm is compact, can be indexed easily, allows inexpensive transfer of information from the printed format, and is economical to duplicate. The step and repeat camera processors which are now available provide an easy way for the library to capture large masses of information, store it cheaply, and retrieve it on demand. Care should be taken to insure that the film produced is of archival quality, but the unknown life of some microforms should not discourage their use. It is better to collect information in a format with a life span of twenty years than not to collect it at all. Although microfilmed periodicals have been used in libraries for quite some time, I find little evidence that public libraries use microfilm in setting up a local data base. I have long believed, however, that the local history resources of a community could have dramatically expanded access if the library could microfilm diaries, letters, and other historical documents that people are not willing to donate to the library. In many instances, the library could increase access to historical documents by offering to microfilm those in the collections of other community agencies. By preserving and keeping safe microfilmed copies of archives in these agencies, the library increases the range of service to them.

It would also be of benefit if the library could microfilm and provide general access to the thousands of appliance and equipment manuals available in the community. The new copyright law apparently permits making one copy of historical materials for preservation purposes and allows a library to copy a copyrighted publication for its own collection if that item is not available on the market. Microfilm could also be used to save storage space for library operational files and materials. Old patron-registration forms could be removed from the drawers and filmed. Materials easily damaged by handling could be made available to all but the serious scholar through microform.

Video Technology

Video technology is a subject very dear to my heart. I will not repeat what has been written by myself and others nor will I expand upon it very much [15, 16, 17]. I do want to make just one point related to the subject of technology and libraries. Like computer costs, the costs of video hardware are continually declining. A two-camera color video system with a three-quarter-inch videotape recorder, audio mixer, microphones, and miscellaneous equipment sells for less than $15,000. A color camera with a Betamax-type recorder is available for less than $2,500. If you watch your local newspaper advertisements, you can pick up a home recorder for less than $600. As more and more homes have video recorders, the need for this format in the public library will increase. This can provide an excellent opportunity for public relations and community involvement. It allows the production of local informational materials, and with cable TV the dissemination of these materials as well as other productions is possible.

Introduction of Technology

Simply adding technologists to our libraries is not the point. Such a staff may allow the library to operate more efficiently and to expand its services, and the presence of technologists may have a positive impact on the librarians, but it will not provide the range of skills needed for overall development. Training library school students in technology or recruiting technologists as faculty for library schools may contribute to the process. Unfortunately, these steps will probably be too slow to be effective. By the time recent graduates have accumulated enough seniority to be able to have much effect in the libraries which employ them, the profession will have been bypassed by other kinds of information providers, and we will have been completely relegated to custodial chores.

To exploit technological potential to the fullest in the public library we must make major changes in our thinking, operations, and, in particular, in our leadership. This may be impossible [18, p. xi]. If it is not, it will take a great deal of motivation, exploration, and implementation. We must translate our own rhetoric into institutional logic. The majority of our profession has difficulty perceiving any role different from what it has known [18, p. 4]. Our present efforts to use technology have affected procedures and work flow but have done little to improve public services. It is difficult to pin down one factor that contributes most to the library's inability to change in order to take on effectively the new role in the library community that many of us think necessary. My own experience in libraries over the last fifteen years leads me to believe that the main problem is the library administrator. A survey by Wasserman indicates that the value judgments of administrators as well as their attitudes are a major impediment to technological change. Most administrators appeared content to let others take the lead in implementing the new technology in libraries [18, p. 117].

Administrators are the hardest pressed and most persistently harassed group in the business world. They can rely no longer on one set of skills to last a career [7, p. 308]. Based on Wasserman's survey, it appears that library administrators have not yet suffered or are unaware of this pressure.

Administrators, then, have the responsibility to promote the ability of our libraries to provide informational service to our communities. They must stop turning up their noses at information and technologies that people need because of format or some academic disdain on their part. They must become aware of the possibilities of technology and should work to increase their own personal abilities to integrate it into the range of tools available to solve problems.

In sum I ask, What is the potential of technology in public libraries? It is to expand traditional functions. It allows the library to capture, publish, store, and retrieve information for the community. With a Xerox and a glue-binding machine, anyone can publish printed material. The technology is not expensive. With a videotape recorder and a camera, anyone can produce audiovisual material. The technology is not expensive. With a step-and-repeat microfiche camera processor, anyone can preserve material for posterity and index it while they are at it. With a computer anyone can organize an inventory of these materials and provide high-speed information services. With just a terminal, a library can access over 100 data bases throughout the country. With these tools the library is not wedded to archaic methods of traditional publishing.

Using available technology the library can make a planned and conscious shift from its traditional supply function to an information and professional advisory function in the service of nonspecialized adults [1, p. 85]. The library can provide the leadership and the focus for communities desperate for leadership in developing information sys-

tems. Library administrators will determine the degree of leadership
provided. There is no doubt in my mind that the electronic library will
become a reality. The main question for us is, Will we be the ones who
design and operate that library?

REFERENCES

 1. Martin, Lowell A. *Adults and the Pratt Library: A Question of the Quality of Life*. Balti-
    more: Enoch Pratt Free Library, 1974.
 2. Dervin, Brenda. "The Everyday Information Needs of the Average Citizen: A
    Taxonomy for Analysis." In *Information for the Community*, edited by Manfred Kochen
    and Joseph C. Donohue. Chicago: American Library Association, 1976.
 3. Sackman, Harold, and Boehm, Barry W., eds. *Planning Community Information Utilities*.
    DIALOG abstract. Montvale, N.J.: American Federation of Information Processing
    Societies, 1972.
 4. Lacy, Dan, and Mathews, Virginia. *Social Change and the Library, 1945–1980. Final
    Report to the National Advisory Commission on Libraries*. DIALOG abstract. Washington,
    D.C.: National Advisory Commission on Libraries, 1967.
 5. Dowlin, Kenneth E., and Fuller, Elisabeth. "Community Information Center: Talk or
    Action?" In *The Use of Computers and Related Reference Activities in Libraries*, edited by F.
    Wilfrid Lancaster. Champaign: University of Illinois Graduate School of Library
    Science, 1976.
 6. Toffler, Alvin. *Future Shock*. New York: Random House, 1970.
 7. McLuhan, Marshall. *Understanding Media: The Extensions of Man*. New York: New
    American Library, 1964.
 8. Anderson, Norm. "Facsimile Speeds Records Transmission." *Information and Records
    Management* 11 (November 1977): 10–11, 37.
 9. *Profile: An All Products Newsletter from the 3M Company*. St. Paul, Minn.: 3M, n.d.
10. DeGennaro, Richard. "Library Automation: Changing Patterns and New Directions."
    DIALOG abstract. *Library Journal* 101 (January 1976): 175–83.
11. Martin, Susan K., and Butler, Brett, eds. *Library Automation: The State of the Art II*.
    Chicago: American Library Association, 1975.
12. Isaacson, Portia. "Personnel Computing." *Datamation* 23 (November 1977): 213–15.
13. Advertisements in *Datamation*, vol. 23 (November 1977).
14. *System Builder's Catalog*. Boston, Winter 1978.
15. *Cable Television and Education: A Report from the Field*. Washington, D.C.: National Cable
    Television Association, 1973.
16. Monroe, Early. "More Futures than One." DIALOG abstract. Speech presented at the
    Federal City College Conference on Cable TV, Washington, D.C.: ERIC Documenta-
    tion Reproduction Service, 1974.
17. Brown, James W. "Public Libraries and the New Media: A Review and References."
    DIALOG abstract. Stanford, Calif.: Stanford University: ERIC Documentation Re-
    production Service, 1975.
18. Wasserman, Paul. *The New Librarianship: A Challenge for Change*. New York: R. R.
    Bowker Co., 1972.

COOPERATION, NETWORKING, AND THE LARGER UNIT IN THE PUBLIC LIBRARY

Genevieve M. Casey

As a part of this conference probing the present circumstances and future prospects of the American public library, I have been asked to explore with you a phenomenon of the twentieth century which most observers consider a major development of the public library: its movement away from autonomous local control and support toward consolidation and cooperation with other public libraries and, more recently, with libraries of other types. I have been asked to consider the dimension, the direction, and the meaning of this movement in terms of its administrative, fiscal, and service implications and to assess how the public library today, as part of a unitype (public library) or a multitype system, fits into the national information network proposed by the National Commission on Libraries and Information Science (NCLIS), or into some other national configuration which may evolve.

In order to discharge this responsibility, I would like first to place the movement toward cooperation or larger units in its historical perspective and, in so doing, to map its range and extent.

A Local Agency

The American public library, a product of the nineteenth century, like its British counterpart, was conceived as a local agency which would be locally supported, locally controlled, and responsive to the needs of its local community, whether school district, village, town, or city. The role of the state was confined to providing the legislative framework enabling local communities to organize and tax themselves for library service. This concept of local control and local support of libraries paralleled our concept of support for elementary and secondary public education. That this somewhat outmoded model of public library organization continues today is evidenced by the most recent edition of the *American Library Directory* [1], which identifies over 8,000 local, somewhat autonomous public libraries, serving communities of less than 1,000 up to several million people. That the traditional pattern of public library structure is alive and well today is further evidenced by the pattern of their support:

82 percent is local, 13 percent is provided by the state, and 5 percent is federal [2].

Despite efforts toward cooperation with other public libraries, and more recently toward affiliation with other types of libraries, such as academic, special, and school, the American public library today is still a local institution. It has to struggle with the same problems of political fragmentation which plague other public services, such as transportation, sanitation, and police and fire protection. Indeed, a study recently conducted under the auspices of the NCLIS characterized the public library today as "an almost randomly distributed pattern of semi-independent local service agencies and systems, only loosely coordinated with other libraries" [3]. This tradition of local autonomy, fiercely defended, has repeatedly been cited as the greatest single barrier to a more rational organization of public library services.

The Early County Library and the Trend toward Larger Units

The movement toward larger units of public library service began early in the twentieth century with the development of county libraries which were intended initially to serve a rural population living outside the scope of village, town, and city libraries. As such, the county libraries themselves were very small units until James Gillis, state librarian of California, began to promote countywide library service as an alternative to small independent libraries. Within five years of a 1911 county library law, thirty-seven of California's fifty-eight counties were persuaded to establish such libraries, and soon thereafter, within the period of Gillis's regime as state librarian, county libraries with 2,441 branches and three-quarters of a million books were serving half a million Californians [4]. County libraries developed rapidly throughout the nation on the California model. According to a summary provided by Charles Nelson in his public library system study [5], county libraries with incomes over $1,000 grew from 225 in 1935 to 651 in 1944, to about 1,000 in 1960. *The American Library Directory* for 1976–77 [1] identifies 1,203 county and multicounty libraries. California's success with consolidated countywide service inspired the recommendation of the first national plan for public libraries, which was issued in 1948, that in the future "the average public library unit . . . should serve a population of about 90,000 and an average of 2,500 square miles" [6].

Extending the concept of the county library as envisioned by James Gillis and the national plan and giving impetus to the idea of the importance of larger units of service were the findings of the Public Library Inquiry, the first (and perhaps last) full-scale investigation of the public library as a social institution [7]. Leigh, director of the inquiry, and his associates emphasized as a major recommendation that to provide adequate service to its community the small public library must affiliate with other public libraries to create larger units of service. The degree to which this recommendation, and the data which supported it, were accepted by public library leadership is suggested by the fact that the Public Library Association's 1955 *Minimum Standards for Public Library Service* in 1966 became the *Minimum Standards for Public Library Systems* [8]. Even in 1955, the standards asserted that its recommendation for a "cooperative approach on the part of libraries is the single most important recommendation of this document" [9].

The Impact of LSA and LSCA

The passage of the Library Service Act (LSA) in 1956 provided the opportunity for library planners to implement their conviction that some new pattern of public library organization was long overdue. LSA, focusing upon improving and extending public library service to rural areas, provided state librarians and their advisor-colleagues with federal funds to plan long-range, statewide programs. Universally, the state plans emphasized linking together local (including county) public libraries into systems in order to provide people access to a wider range of materials and to the services of more qualified personnel.

State-supported public library systems launched by New York in 1958 provided a model, adopted with some variation, for most, if not all, of the emerging public library systems under LSA. The New York systems were based upon nine fundamental assumptions: (1) Responsibility for public library support and control is and should continue to be local. (2) The state has an obligation to support regional library systems in order to strengthen and equalize local library service. (3) State (or federally) funded regional library systems should supplement, not supplant, local public libraries—indeed, they should serve as incentives for increased local support. (4) Regional library systems should protect the autonomy of the local library, leaving intact the authority of its trustees to control policy, budget, and personnel. (5) Regional systems should be governed by trustees representative of the region and of the local member libraries, and these trustees should have the authority to choose those services of most value for the region. (6) Certain central services, such as acquisition, cataloging, classification and processing of materials, purchase of supplies, and staff development can be performed more economically on a regional rather than a local basis. (7) The capacity of the local library to serve its users can be enhanced by—indeed, is dependent upon—access to a strong central headquarters collection as well as to materials in all member libraries. (8) The expertise of specialists in such

areas as children and youth services, audiovisual materials and programs, buildings, and management can be shared by several public
libraries. (9) Library service in large, sparsely populated areas is more
expensive to maintain than service to the same number of users in
densely populated areas.

Within the context of these assumptions, the New York State funding
formula was based on the overall population of the system's region plus
its size (number of square miles). It carried an incentive for maintenance
of local support by all member libraries. Other than the general
provision that to qualify for funding a system needed to serve a region
with at least 200,000 people and that it needed to submit a plan for
regional service acceptable to the state library agency, the New York
system law placed responsibility for determining services and policies for
the systems upon the regional system board, which was elected by and
from trustees of the local member libraries. The major activities of the
New York systems, according to a study completed in 1966 [10],
clustered around acquisition and technical processing of materials,
sharing of resources (interlibrary loan and interlibrary reference), and
staff development.

With the exception of Hawaii, which maintains a unique, statewide
public library system, and New Mexico, which operates a statewide
service aimed at otherwise unserved populations, all states in their plans
for the expenditure of federal funds under LSA and its successor, the
Library Services and Construction Act (LSCA), have focused on the
creation of public library systems more or less on the New York model.

The Nelson Study

In 1967–68 Charles Nelson undertook his massive study of multijurisdictional *Public Library Systems in the United States* [5]. This was commissioned by the Public Library Association. The objectives of the study
were (1) to collect information on multijurisdictional public library
systems throughout the country, especially on their governmental-
legal-administrative structure, base of financial support, materials and
resources, personnel, and services; (2) to compare, for a sample of such
systems, the financing and services provided by the system, with the aim
of assessing the success to date of the system concept; (3) to reveal, by
means of intensive analysis of six selected systems, the most critical
problems in system development and some of the possible alternative
solutions; and (4) to propose a framework of policy guidelines on future
system development for further consideration by the Public Library
Association and the ALA.

The study was able to identify 1,159 systems in operation before

January 1, 1964, an inventory acknowledged to be incomplete. Although the Nelson study is of fundamental importance as a benchmark, it left many questions unanswered, not because of defects in research design but because data were simply not available. The study, for example, could not document that the regional approach reduces (or does not) reduce costs to the taxpayer. It could not answer the question of optimal system size in population or in square miles. It could not document whether an administrative or organizational pattern was superior. The data gathered did support, however, the following conclusions about public library systems: (1) Systems do provide users with increased access to library resources and services; (2) systems succeed in extending library services to a significant number of previously unserved people; and (3) systems foster an "increased professionalism," that is, a higher standard of cataloging, a more competent reference service, etc. In analyzing problems which impeded the effectiveness of systems, the study concluded that (1) a combination of weak libraries does not make a strong system; (2) there is a direct ratio between the number of services offered by a system and the size of its population, but little or no correlation with size of system area; (3) systems have difficulty in bringing in hold-out libraries, an acute problem when the nonaffiliated library is a large one upon which quality system services depend; (4) only a minority of systems have ties to libraries outside the system, except for the state library; (5) inadequate training on the job, especially as evidenced by lack of knowledge of the resources of the system, accounts for more failures in reference service than any other single factor; and (6) in systems adjoining or including a major city, there is a pervasive need for an equitable means of reimbursement to the city, which usually supports a strong library serving many patrons from outside its border [5, pp. 241–64].

Activities of public library systems, as documented by the Nelson study, and also by *Emerging Library Systems* [10] in New York, tend to be acquisition and technical processing of materials, interlibrary loan and reference, and staff development. Within the last ten years, the advent of the Ohio College Library Center (OCLC) and other systems of shared cataloging have tended to minimize (or change) the technical processing functions of public library systems and further emphasize their resource sharing.

By the mid-sixties, unitype public library systems were in place to some degree in most states. The *ASLA Report on Interlibrary Cooperation* [11], in 1976, identified thirty-one states with formally organized public library systems, regularly funded through the state library agency. State support of public library systems ranged from $25,000 in Idaho to $24,810,000 in New York. Ten states (California, Georgia, Illinois, Massachusetts, Michigan, Minnesota, New York, North Carolina,

Pennsylvania, and Wisconsin) were currently providing over $1,000,000 in statutory state aid to public library systems.

The Emergence of the Multitype Library System

About ten years ago, three converging factors led to the creation of a new "generation" of library cooperation: the multitype library systems with academic, special, institutional, and school libraries. The first factor was the exponentially increasing human record, coupled with skyrocketing costs and tightening budgets which caused public, academic, and special libraries to realize that the sharing of resources was inevitable.

The second factor was the development of a technology capable of overcoming some of the major obstacles to multitype library coordination—geographic distance and that diversity of method which grows out of diversity of mission. Machine Readable Cataloging (MARC), the capability of recording catalog copy on magnetic tape, susceptible to machine manipulation and transmission over telephone lines, was the enormous intellectual breakthrough underlying much of the progress in multitype library networks. Leadership in using MARC to build cooperative bibliographic data banks came first from large academic and research libraries where the pressures of the expanding record were felt most sharply, but increasingly, large public libraries and public library systems have joined shared-cataloging cooperatives.

A major development as a result of MARC was OCLC, chartered in 1967 as a not-for-profit computerized system to link together all the resources in the state colleges and universities of Ohio. Its primary product, based on the MARC tapes, was the provision of cataloging copy with a by-product of location information. Within ten years, OCLC has spread from the publicly supported academic libraries of Ohio to over 700 libraries nationwide, largely academic and public. The initial cost of joining OCLC, about half of which is a fixed cost regardless of how many libraries are in the system, has proved a strong incentive for many large libraries to cooperate with each other. OCLC has demonstrated (1) that shared cataloging need not require rigid standardization (individual library users can alter the record almost at will); (2) that an on-line system can save cataloging time; and, consequently, (3) that it can at least hold the line on cost.

The enormous data bank which has been building in the Columbus computer as a by-product of shared cataloging can also serve as a location tool of major value for interlibrary loan. Under a grant through the Ohio State Library in 1977, OCLC now has developed the capacity for hierarchical display of location marks, that is, a display first of locations of any given title within a region, then of locations in the region, then in the state, and finally in the nation. Although most of the OCLC records are for titles published within the last ten years, numerous studies have indicated that these are the materials most often requested in libraries of all types. With the rapid spread of OCLC, as well as similar and essentially compatible systems such as BALLOTS, headquartered at Stanford University in California, we seem well on the way toward a national multitype library network.

The third factor which has encouraged public library systems to enter into multitype networks was the enactment of Title III of LSCA in 1966. Title III provided funds through state libraries to "establish and maintain local, regional, state or interstate networks of libraries for the systematic and effective coordination of the resources of school, public, academic and special libraries or special information centers." The legislation required that all types of libraries in a state should collaborate in developing a comprehensive statewide plan for access to all of the state's resources. Funds could be spent for planning, equipment, personnel, rental of space, and communication but not for materials—a prohibition which forced the linkage of existing resources.

Despite the minimal funding it has received, Title III has contributed significantly to the development of multitype, statewide, and regional cooperatives. Activities in most states have focused on interlibrary loan and reference networks, for which the major public and academic libraries in the state or region are used as resource libraries. In the five-year plans for the period 1972–77, required for eligibility for LSCA funds, all states now have included plans for establishing or extending multitype interlibrary loan reference networks. The 1976–77 *American Library Directory* [1] lists 350 "Networks, Consortia and Other Cooperative Organizations," of which 133 include public libraries. The ASLA study in 1975 identified thirty-one states with multitype library networks, regularly funded by the state library agency [11]. Although network configurations differ from state to state, most multitype networks are designed ultimately for shared cataloging based on the MARC record and for interlibrary loan and reference. A review of multitype systems in two key states may highlight similarities and differences.

The New York System
New York, a leader in the development of public library systems, has also developed the prototype for a layered organizational pattern for the coordination of all the resources in all types of libraries in the state. In nine large geographic regions covering the state, New York now funds nine 3R (Reference-Research-Resource) councils. These are not libraries, but rather service organizations designed to facilitate the sharing of resources among all public, academic, special, and school libraries. Membership for the local library, as in the public library systems, is

voluntary. As the name implies, the 3R's are intended to meet reference and research needs beyond the capacity of local libraries and library systems. Most 3R systems include several public library systems, one or more campuses of the State University of New York, and several community colleges, private colleges and universities, and special libraries. Although the character and configuration of the region determine the program for each 3R council, activity generally has concentrated upon interlibrary loan and reference. Metro 3R, serving libraries in the five boroughs of New York City, plus libraries in Westchester County and New Jersey, has moved into cooperative acquisition of rare and expensive items, computerized organization of materials, and also instituted a strong program of staff development. Entrance for the user to the 3R system is commonly through his local academic or public library. 3R councils are funded by state grants, which are authorized by a line in the state budget rather than by statute. Legislation to authorize state funding according to a formula based upon the number of professional workers and postsecondary students within each 3R region has not yet been enacted. Most councils currently supplement their state grants from other sources, such as membership fees and foundation grants.

At the top level in New York is NYSIL (New York State Interlibrary Loan), a state-funded system which ties together the state library and the major research libraries in the state to meet the demand for research materials that are not available in the public library systems or in the academic or special library affiliates of the regional councils. Entrance to NYSIL is through the 3R councils. NYSIL members are compensated by the state for items searched and/or supplied. In summary, the New York system is based on a layered approach with an interface between strong public library systems, the state university system, the state library, and other libraries in the state.

The degree to which New York's layered, interfacing network works in placing materials in the hands of its users is illustrated by table 1, drawn from Neff's study relating to the Rochester region, which is served by the Pioneer Public Library System and the Rochester 3R Council [12, p. 92]. That New York's complex layered system develops some overlap is documented by tables 2 and 3 from Neff's study of the Rochester regions [12, pp. 92–93].

The conclusions reached by Neff as she attempted to evaluate the performance of the New York system in Rochester may summarize what the New York plan can teach the library profession about multitype library networks:

The New York Mixed experience, better known as the 3R's, has demonstrated the validity of serving the nation's library needs through cooperative coordina-

TABLE 1
ROCHESTER AREA INTERLIBRARY LOAN STATISTICS—CALENDAR 1975

Total Loan Requests	N	%
From public library outlets:	73,857	100.0
Filled by public libraries	65,559	88.7
Filled by RRRLC (academic-special) libraries*	1,857	2.5
Filled by NYSIL statewide network	4,487	6.1
Requests not filled†	1,954	2.7
From academic-special libraries:	34,793	100.0
Filled by public libraries	2,527	7.3
Filled by RRRLC academic-special libraries	22,360	64.2
Filled by NYSIL statewide network	4,284	12.3
Filled by NLM network	290	.9
Requests not filled†	5,332	15.3

NOTE.—RRRLC = 3R Library Council; NLM = National Library of Medicine.

* Of a total of 3,811 requests channeled into the RRRLC network, 1,857, or 48.7 percent were filled.

† Not filled: materials were not available or requests were not referred to supplying libraries because of user deadlines.

TABLE 2
SUMMARY OF SIMILAR SERVICES EACH TYPE OF COOPERATIVE OFFERS ITS MEMBERS

Service	Pioneer System	Rochester Council
Delivery	All members	Ten largest only
Interlibrary loan	All members	All members
Regional library borrowing card	All members	Partial only
Continuing education programs	Extensive	Limited
Media materials	All types	16 mm film only
Centralized processing	Complete	None
Publications	Numerous	Few

TABLE 3
SUMMARY OF DIFFERENT SERVICES EACH TYPE OF COOPERATIVE OFFERS ITS MEMBERS

Service	Pioneer System	Rochester Council
Book and film programs	Many	None
Bookmobile	As needed	None
Translations	None	By referral
Union list of serials	None	Most libraries included
Patent copying service	None	Fee service
Technical and business information (literature search service)	None	Arranged through free-lance searchers

tion of many types of library collections and services. In the Rochester area it has proved the following:

Librarians from diverse types of libraries are interested in learning together, planning together, and working together to implement their plans.

Small and large libraries can make contributions each at their own levels.

Users are willing to pay for specialized services tailored to their unique needs.

Owners of large collections who act as major suppliers need to be reimbursed for the labor and the materials in a "net supplier" situation.

Inventiveness, imagination, and compromise in devising cooperative arrangements will overcome most impediments.

One of the key ingredients to success is money, in the millions of dollars range at the state and multistate levels. Without realistic funding, participants' enthusiasms wilt, expectations are not fulfilled, and the entire effort is jeopardized. [12, p. 96]

The Illinois System

Illinois, in contrast to New York, has built its multitype library coordination on a nucleus of unitype—in this case, public library—systems. In 1965 Illinois passed its Library Systems Act, which created eighteen multipurpose regional public library systems which now have a membership on a voluntary basis of almost all of Illinois's 555 local public libraries. These public library systems, like New York's, are state funded, locally controlled by boards elected by the trustees of member libraries, and chartered or approved by the state library. Unlike New York's public library system law, however, Illinois's Public Library System Act designated four major libraries (the University of Illinois at Urbana-Champaign, the University of Southern Illinois, the Chicago Public Library, and the Illinois State Library) as research and reference centers and authorized the state library to designate additional libraries with special subject strengths as "special resource centers."

In order to coordinate resources in all Illinois libraries and to make them universally available, the Library Systems Act also authorized nonpublic libraries to become "affiliate" (that is, nonvoting) members of the systems. Nonpublic libraries are required to sign a "memorandum of agreement," which affirms their obligation to meet the current ongoing library needs of their own clientele from their own resources, to honor the Illinois Regional Interlibrary Loan Code (a more liberal version of the national interlibrary code), to consent to lend materials as a supplementary source, and to provide data on interlibrary loan to the state library for use in evaluating the systems. Responsibility for promoting affiliate membership lies with the eighteen public library systems.

In 1973, the state library began a special effort to phase other types of libraries into the systems by making a two-year LSCA grant to each of the eighteen public library systems for hiring library cooperation specialists. In general, Illinois has proved reasonably successful in folding academic libraries into its public library systems but less successful in persuading special and school libraries that they have anything to gain from the network. By March 1974, after over a year of effort, only 12 percent of Illinois's special libraries had joined, and by mid-1975, only 103 school libraries out of Illinois's 1,039 school districts had joined.

Barriers to affiliation that seem to be a concern on the part of academic libraries are that they will be inundated by interlibrary loan requests from the system (although in fact, this has not been a problem), a preference by both academic and special libraries for their own formal type of library arrangements, and the usual conviction that the local library has everything it needs. The indifference of the majority of school libraries in Illinois to participation in multitype library systems is typical of school libraries throughout the nation.

The Illinois Regional Library Council
In 1971, another kind of multitype cooperative sprang up in Illinois, parallel to the state sponsored and funded library systems: the Illinois Regional Library Council. This was initiated in the six-county Chicago metropolitan area and includes five public library systems, which serve over 7 million people and hundreds of special and academic libraries. As of 1975, the council's membership was 40 percent special libraries, 25 percent academic libraries, 29 percent public libraries, and 6 percent school libraries. Funding is from LSCA and member fees. The council's purpose is to facilitate in-person access to all collections in the area by means of an INFOPASS and to facilitate interlibrary loan by the coordination of existing delivery systems and by the publication of a directory, *Libraries and Information Centers in the Chicago Metropolitan Area,* which lists subject strengths, special collections, hours open, and lending policies of the major libraries in the council.

The regional council in Chicago has proposed but not yet achieved statutory recognition from the state, which would provide it with a per capita funding formula. Just how the regional council will fit into Illinois's objective, as expressed by its former state librarian, Alphonse Trezza, to achieve "a single system representative of all types of libraries in the eighteen regions of the state" [13, p. 400] remains somewhat obscure. Probably no viable pattern can be devised in any state which eliminates overlap completely. Metropolitan regional councils, similar to Illinois's, now exist in Ohio, California, Minnesota, and many other states, all initiated within the last ten years, all multitype, all designed to facilitate access to all collections in the area, all with a staff development component, and a few with programs of shared acquisition.

States where both unitype and multitype coordination is not as far advanced have the opportunity now to build upon the experience of pioneer states and to take advantage of technological tools not previously available. OCLC and similar bibliographic data banks providing on-line cataloging and an on-line, hierarchical location tool, can now provide more flexibility to the planners of library cooperation. Local libraries which call on their terminals information on all locations within a state or nation need not channel requests through a central library of a network or maintain expensive and sometimes inefficient union catalogs, book catalogs, etc. Area technical processing centers, which have consumed a substantial part of the millions of dollars from New York State chan-neled into public library systems, can now be replaced with single-state or multistate contracts with OCLC or similar bibliographic centers. Smaller libraries can depend upon MARC-based cataloging and processing from jobbers.

In general, the experience of other pioneer states has documented that (1) the primary services of library systems perceived as the most essential are interlibrary loan and reference; (2) local and system staff development is the key to system performance (performance meaning that the user is provided with what he wants, where and when he needs it); (3) administrative costs, whether defrayed directly by actual local, state, and/or federal funds or indirectly by in-kind services, are a major cost of system services, while administrative costs tend to grow as funds are available; (4) system structure (that is, personnel, buildings, equipment, etc.) can inhibit the capacity of systems to take advantage of new technological advances; (5) structures designed to preserve local autonomy can be costly in time and money; (6) tying together similar collections in public libraries cannot meet the needs of a total community—therefore, multitype rather than, or in addition to, unitype library systems are clearly the wave of the immediate future; and (7) per capita formulas for the support of library systems do not lend themselves to evaluation or accountability.

Future Administrative Patterns

Building upon the experience of public library systems and their successors, the multitype systems, the library profession needs to search for new patterns of administration and support of library systems. For administration, we need to devise structures with a maximum of flexibility, equity, and economy. We need to ask ourselves what systems are for. The answer, at least at present, is clear: systems are for resource sharing, that is, interlibrary loan and reference, with eventual shared acquisition; for shared cataloging as a way of holding the line on, if not reducing, cost; and for staff development. Technology such as OCLC plus a sensible plan for reimbursing resource libraries may minimize much of the administrative superstructure previously thought necessary for system functioning. Ideally, it seems to me that systems of the future should be as structureless as possible and should have maximum potential for taking advantage of new technology as it emerges, with minimum dollars and time expended in administration. Opportunity for local member libraries to monitor systems and to determine services is indispensable; but we have yet to decide, or even to face the question of, how much participatory management a library system can afford and how much it can afford to neglect. The answer can be found in a clear, consistent vision of what systems are about, that is, improved library and information service to users and potential users of local libraries.

The library profession also needs to develop a more philosophically defensible and more practical and accountable way to fund library systems. As far back as 1934, Lowell Martin proposed a partnership in the funding of public libraries by local, state, and federal government. No library planner today believes that the local community should support all public library service, especially areawide service, and many states have now assumed some responsibility for equalizing library service and encouraging public library systems. Moreover, with the reenactment of LSCA for another five years, Congress has recently reaffirmed some federal responsibility for the support of public libraries. Nevertheless, the question of what the relative role should be of each level of government for the support and control of libraries and library systems remains unclear.

It is clear that local communities cannot and will not undertake the support of regional library systems, no matter how beneficial they are, and that public library service locally affordable is and will continue to be inadequate and uneven. It is equally clear that academic libraries cannot and will not divert their often shrinking funds to provide back-up resources for the whole community. It could be argued that the state, in the role of equalizing educational opportunity, has a responsibility to share in the cost of operating local public libraries, as well as to share in or shoulder significantly the cost of area- or statewide library coopera-tives. It could be argued that the federal government, which consumes most tax revenues, should share some of that revenue for the operation of local public libraries as well as statewide systems, although revenue sharing has proven to be a disappointment to most public libraries. And it could be argued, as NCLIS has, that the communication links which connect library resources within each state to the national information system are the responsibility of the federal government.

What constitutes a fair share for each level of government remains to be defined by the library profession. This definition is contingent upon what we conceive to be the role of each library in each level of the network.

Whatever the sources of funding for library systems, we need to find more defensible allocation formulae than the per capita basis. It may be that the data we now have about the costs and patterns of use of interlibrary loan and reference could help us to devise a formula for cooperative ventures based on unit interloan costs, which take into consideration fair compensation to providing libraries and the use of communication and delivery systems, as well as the cost of the staff development necessary at all levels.

Summary

In summary, the library profession, as it moves toward new patterns and new generations of library organization, needs to keep its eye firmly fixed on the reason all American libraries exist: making the record of human experience in all its forms genuinely accessible to all Americans, no matter where they live or how well or ill educated they are or with what libraries they are or are not affiliated. Within that user context, the profession needs to seek new patterns of library cooperation which are effective, flexible, economically feasible, and equitable.

Specific activities for library consortia, as defined recently by John Knapp, seem, with one exception, adequate for the here and now: "Shared access to collections through enhanced interlibrary loan service and broadened scope of borrowing privileges. Coordinated collection development to avoid duplication of materials in areas which do not serve the primary interests or research needs of local library clientele. Shared access to bibliographic data in support of library technical services" [14, p. 133]. To these, I would add a fourth goal, the development of staff. As NCLIS emphasized in their document, *Toward a National Program*: "To achieve a technological organizational upgrading of libraries and information centers will require new approaches to recruitment, personnel development, continuing education, technical training, trustee orientation and other matters relating to human resources" [15, p. 44].

In his early study of the manpower implications of the movement of libraries toward systems, Edwin Olson defined some of the varied expertise needed for future development. We shall need, he concluded, "persons who are acquainted with experimental design, statistics, and mathematics who can develop complex system models [necessary to] intricate planning [and also] politically sophisticated persons who can innovatively adapt procedures and effectively deal with the rapidly changing environment" [16, p. 81].

The "Mission Statement for Public Libraries" [17], issued by the Public Library Association in 1977 as part of guidelines for the last quarter of the twentieth century, provides a clear mandate for continued public library cooperation with the libraries. Redefining certain key words used in describing traditional public library standards, the mission statement declares that "*access* now implies innovative, imaginative delivery techniques which overcome geographic, educational, physical and psychological barriers, as well as convenient location and hours open. *Community* means not only a narrow geographic service support area, but also the wider area—regional, state, national and international—to which every local library must be connected. *Library system* means the affiliation of libraries of all types" [17, pp. 617–18].

The public library of the future, as envisioned by the "Mission Statement," would (1) provide access to the human records of the past, factual, imaginative, scientific and humanistic, partly through its own collections, and partly through an effective network linking all collections in the region, state, nation, and the world; (2) develop, in cooperation with other information agencies and libraries, a responsible policy about preserving and erasing portions of humankind's voluminous current record and negotiate a consensus about the criteria for judging between materials which are significant or representative and those which are trivial or redundant; (3) in the light of this responsibility to preserve or to erase, assume leadership in defining a new statement of professional ethics and in creating new structures to protect intellectual freedom; (4) assume a leadership role in coordinating the acquisition policies of other libraries and information agencies, because no one agency can be expected to preserve all significant and representative materials in all forms, at all levels; and (5) having developed policies for shared acquisition, assume leadership in creating and maintaining an effective network so that all citizens would have easy access to any record, no matter where it was stored [17, pp. 619–20].

In conclusion, the "Mission Statement" asserts that "it is only through linkages with other more specialized libraries and information agencies that the totality of the public library mission can be accomplished. The public library assumes leadership responsibility with the state library and other regional and national organizations for linking community resources to other resources in the state, nation and the world" [17, p. 620].

In its movement toward unitype and multitype library systems, the public library now has a substantial body of experience upon which to build. New technological tools are now available to deal with many of the barriers against more rational organization. One can be certain, in our rapidly changing world, that new structures will be devised, like and unlike those of the first seventy-five years of the twentieth century. That we have not yet found all the answers is self-evident. That exciting new frontiers lie ahead is equally certain.

REFERENCES

1. *The American Library Directory*, 1976–1977. 30th ed. New York: R. R. Bowker Co., 1976.
2. Government Studies and Systems, Inc. *Improving State Aid to Public Libraries*. Washington, D.C.: National Commission on Libraries and Information Science, 1977.
3. Government Studies and Systems, Inc. *Alternatives for Financing the Public Library*. Washington, D.C.: National Commission on Libraries and Information Science, 1974.
4. Garceau, Oliver. *The Public Library in the Political Process: A Report of the Public Library Inquiry*. New York: Columbia University Press, 1949.

5. Charles Nelson and Associates. *Public Library Systems in the United States: A Survey of Multijurisdictional Systems.* Chicago: American Library Association, 1969.
6. Joeckel, C. B., and Winslow, Amy. *A National Plan of Public Library Service.* Chicago: American Library Association, 1948.
7. Leigh, Robert D. *The Public Library in the United States.* New York: Columbia University Press, 1950.
8. Public Library Association. *Minimum Standards for Public Library Systems.* Chicago: American Library Association, 1966.
9. Public Library Association. *Public Library Service: A Guide to Evaluation, with Minimum Standards.* Chicago: American Library Association, 1956.
10. *Emerging Library Systems: The 1963–66 Evaluation of the New York State Public Library Systems.* Albany, N.Y.: University of the State of New York, State Education Department, Division of Evaluation, 1967.
11. ASLA Interlibrary Cooperation Subcommittee, eds. *The ASLA Report on Interlibrary Cooperation.* Chicago: Association of State Library Agencies, 1976.
12. Neff, Evaline B. "New York Case Study 1: Rochester—A Rural/Urban Mix." In *Multitype Library Cooperation*, edited by Beth A. Hamilton and William B. Ernst, Jr. New York: R. R. Bowker Co., 1977.
13. "Advancing Illinet: Anticipation and Expectation of the Future." *Illinois Libraries* 57 (June 1975): 396–414.
14. Knapp, John. "Requirement for the National Library Network." *Journal of Library Automation* 10 (June 1977): 131–400.
15. *Toward a National Program for Library and Information Services: Goals for Action.* Washington, D.C.: National Commission on Libraries and Information Science, 1975.
16. Olson, Edwin. *Interlibrary Cooperation.* Washington, D.C.: Office of Education, Bureau of Research, 1970.
17. "A Mission Statement for Public Libraries." *American Libraries* 8 (December 1977): 615–20.

THE FUTURE OF REFERENCE AND INFORMATION SERVICE IN THE PUBLIC LIBRARY

Thomas Childers

At a certain point in history the public library could have been accurately characterized as an institution devoted primarily to storing documents, circulating them, and providing facilities for their use on site—an institution essentially without "reference service" as a formally stated mission. As the institution evolved, reference service and the provision of information—a guidance mission—became formalized. Gates has said recently: "Reference work in the public library emphasizes facts, information, ideas, interpretation, and personal aid. It provides, in person and by telephone, practical information to be used immediately, and it provides resources and aid in study and research" [1, p. 149]. This picture of modern public library reference and information service, to the extent that it is accurate, has come about as the result of forces acting on the public library as a social institution. The picture will change or not change in the years to come, depending on how these forces continue to act.

There have been changes in the past. There has been growth in the number and occasional improvement in the quality of reference documents and indexes. There have been technological innovations that had potential for change: the telephone and microforms. There have been changes in library organization—such as the increase in consolidated library systems—that have probably resulted in stronger question-answering capabilities. Developments in recent years suggest further changes that may be in the offing.

Some of the changes discussed in this paper have already taken place in isolated public library agencies. On-line search services, information and referral (I & R), large reference and information networks, and measurement of reference performance can be found in some places. While these are certainly innovations in a given public library agency, it would be premature to view them as accomplished changes in the public library institution. In the following pages I shall first deal with forces for change in reference and information work in the public library institution: politics and economics, society and the individual, the profession, technology, and the growth of information. Second, I shall draw brief sketches of some possible futures for the service in individual libraries.

Let us first consider some of the major forces for change in the future of reference and information service.

Politics and Economics

1. *Diminished Use*

The diminished use that some libraries, particularly inner-city libraries, faced in the 1960s and 1970s has been documented often. Scores of these libraries—as well as others which were not directly affected by losses in readership—responded by "reaching out" to new users with both traditional and nontraditional services. Clearly, this effort to change was intended to benefit the client. Just as clearly, it was intended to build for public libraries a stronger political and economic base. It is an example of the profession's search (1) to attract great numbers of erstwhile nonusers and make them vocal library advocates, and (2) to attract the attention of the governors and funders of libraries and make them library supporters. Some reference and information activity in recent years has also been a form of reaching out and has been directed to these ends.

As one example, the growth of I & R service in public libraries has apparently been stimulated by, among other things, the search for a service with high impact on nonusers and, through them and the related publicity, on the governing and funding bodies, including boards of trustees, local officials, and the voters. This is best demonstrated in the Five Cities Neighborhood Information Centers Project. Partly as a result of participating in an I & R consortium with four other cities, Houston Public Library won substantial increases in its budget. In Detroit, another of the five cities, I & R appears to have been responsible for retaining some funds in the library's budget during a period of massive budget cuts in all city services [2].

Increased emphasis on special reference and information services to municipal government has also been a direct response to the library's search for greater political and economic power. An attempt has been made to bring the services of the library directly to bear on the problems of the people who control the library's fiscal resources. The value of on-line bibliographic services for solving the problems of city governance could be used as an argument for subscribing to such services [3].

2. *Fiscal Limitations*

The fiscal limitations that many public libraries face and expect to face for the long-term future hold implications for reference and information services. Financial expediency may help propel some libraries toward a cooperative question-answering service such as the pooling represented by the Bay Area Reference Center, or a centralized service such as Library-Line, a statewide reference service for the residents of Connecticut [4]. Concentration of this kind, even though perhaps stimulated by adversity, could have a positive yield by replacing many weak reference and information service points with a few strong ones. From the research done to date (for example [5]), I would anticipate that the library with more staff and document resources and with a higher volume of transactions would provide better reference and information service.

Less positively, shrinking library budgets may mean that expensive services—such as compiling extensive bibliographies, providing on-line bibliographic services or on-line access to data banks, or offering computer time for personal (nonlibrary, nonbibliographic) use —will either not be provided or will be provided at a direct charge to the user. The profession will be faced with a policy choice: offer less than a complete line of user services, or offer certain services only to clients who can and will pay for them. The profession may continue to direct its energies toward guiding clients to documents that are readily available rather than toward seeking the information the client needs regardless of his ability to pay, regardless of his willingness or ability to do the actual searching for himself, regardless of the source or form of the information. The professional view of what constitutes reference and information service may not broaden. Instead, economic exigencies may cause the profession to maintain traditional limitations on the form (print documents) and whereabouts (very local) of the resources made available to the client and the process (professional person consulting local printed documents) that leads to reference and information service.

3. The Market

The market for information services appears to have been growing rapidly in recent years [6], as have the services themselves. Within the last ten to fifteen years this country has witnessed rapid growth of information brokers and information-on-demand enterprises, increased specialization of the media—particularly periodical literature—the emergence of many special purpose I & R services, the development of new home entertaining/informing media, the improvement of biblio-graphic control devices such as indexes and current awareness services. All of these can be expected to compete to some degree with the public library in its reference and information mission: like a library, they all facilitate the individual's access to information. Paradoxically, some of these "competing" developments, when used by the library, can also enhance its services. The Social Science Citation Index, an information and referral manual developed by a local health and welfare council, and highly specialized journals are examples of this.

"It cannot be taken for granted that nineteenth-century means and institutions are the only equitable or economic ways to build and share the information resources of a democracy" [6, p. 10]. In fact, it is clear that nineteenth-century means do not suffice. The share of the information marketplace that the public sector has controlled in the past has been steadily diminishing. It is not likely that an institution such as the public library will regain its prior strength in serving the public's general information needs. However, it is likely that the large public library could continue to be a useful reference source through the deep retrospective collections that it has been building for decades [6]. The public library could become preeminent in storing and retrieving information about the community and its resources, as well as about government services. Other public agencies will probably maintain ascendancy in specific areas, such as the census, assorted social data banks, and medical bibliography. Nonetheless, as fairly recent experience tells us, public sector monopolies will be increasingly limited and will be balanced by or infringed upon by private enterprise in areas such as manipulation of census data, bibliographic data bases of the journal and report literature, abstracting services, and publishing. It is obvious that, even though public libraries will be able to exert the traditional influence of a customer on the information entrepreneur, the future of reference and information work in public libraries will be tied to the star of private information enterprise more than it has been in the past [7]. Should they occur, cataclysms in our economic and legal system, such as statutory prohibition of making a profit from public information, may counteract such a trend. Also, if the citizenry demands that access to all information be publicly supported, the public library may find itself more a master of private information enterprise than its customer. Neither of these futures seems very likely, however.

The Needs of the Individual and Society

Political and economic forces leading to change are inescapable. They have always helped direct the course of library services and always will. On the other hand, the actual needs of the individual and society have to date played an indirect role, at best, in shaping reference and information services. Several studies over the years have indicated that, when asked, individuals will reply that they need a bit more and a bit better of what they already have [8–12]. This kind of data, collected by asking individuals directly about their needs, does not provide the library profession with much insight into the reference and information needs of society. The data have usually been limited in one or both of the following ways: the individual is viewed only in the context of his use or nonuse of library services, or the "information needs" studied are only document-based needs.

More recent studies have disclosed the subtlety and complexity of the individual's information-related needs, the things that motivate him to seek information, his patterns of information seeking, and the ways he uses information retrieved—and even information not retrieved. Through a few of these studies it has become known that the individual's information needs are complex, manifold, everchanging; that he has a strong drive to make sense of things; that he chooses to make sense in a variety of ways, only one of which is seeking external information about the subject of his need; that he makes sense of things at his own speed, in his own way, almost regardless of outside (professional) attempts to influence him; that many of his needs are satisfied through "information" that is not found in documents [13]. Moreover, it has become clear that as our society has increased in complexity the individual has developed an ever more urgent need to find his way through the myriad resources of society toward solutions to his everyday problems [13–15]. This knowledge about the individual could lead the profession to foster more open information transactions with the client in order to accommodate not only his document-related needs, but also his need to inform himself through contact with other human beings, with unpublished files, or with an "experience" or activity. Many public libraries are responding, in part, by establishing some form of I & R.

Professional Norms and Values

Most of the forces that act upon an institution—such as the political, economic, individual, and societal ones discussed above—can act regressively, statically, or progressively. A "profession" is probably a force for stasis more often than not. Professional norms and values tend to solidify professional practice, to keep things as they have been, to counter the impact of external change as much as possible, to maintain internal balance, not necessarily balance with the outside world [16]. Yet there are factors within the library profession that may stimulate change in the reference and information services that public libraries provide and change in the policies that rule the services as well.

1. *Service Policies*
Reference and information service policy has been shown to be uneven. Even within a given reference department, it would not be unusual to find two of the service staff harboring quite divergent ideas about the

services that clients are entitled to [17, 18]. To some, this is evidence of a true profession, inasmuch as the "professional" alone determines the nature (quality) of the transaction [19]. It could also be seen as a normless condition resulting in uneven service. In the latter light, it would appear that matters which should have been settled through formal policy have been left to individual whim and that each librarian within a given library is creating his own set of policies for determining such matters as when to make a long-distance call, whether an in-person query or a telephone query gets priority, and how long to work on a particular question.

There are, however, forces at work that may be precipitating the formation of more explicit reference and information service policy for the library agency. First, restricted reference and information service budgets may be forcing a reconsideration of how much of the library's resources should be expended on a client's questions and which client's questions should be dealt with. Libraries may be compelled to define narrowly, through policy statements, who their clients are and what their legitimate entitlements are. A library that once upon a time was unconcerned about where a user lived may be compelled to restrict service to local tax-paying citizens. A library that used to compile some custom-made bibliographies (not through an automated system) may terminate such a time-consuming service.

Second, studies of reference and information service continue; moreover, the practice of locally collecting reference and information statistics grows. Because of both, the profession has an improved level of knowledge about its performance. The number of studies of the quality of reference and information output has grown since 1968 [5, 20–22]. A recently completed study at Rutgers University begins to offer new insight into the so-called reference interview [23]. Such an investigation helps to dispel myths of performance about the reference transaction and can help bring policy into line with actual practice, or alter practice so that it is brought nearer to policy. It is my experience that early unobtrusive studies of reference performance have not only prompted further investigations on the local level but have impelled some librarians to revise their reference and information processes and policies.

2. Guiding Use

Over the years public librarianship has moved well beyond protecting books from people and into guiding people's use of documentary resources—especially those located in house. The field has yet to establish the provision of information, regardless of form or whereabouts, as anything more than a professional boast. However, the I & R and on-line services provided by a growing number of libraries may indicate a movement away from the document-bound and intramural service that prevails today. Will these new services reform traditional library services? Again, while there is no systematic study of the matter, I hypothesize four new developments from personal observation. (1) In order to reduce "connect time" and save money, librarians who have mediated on-line searches have significantly sharpened their control of the information transaction (that is, "question negotiation" or the "reference interview"). (2) The information transaction has been "opened up" significantly in the case of librarians who have become involved with I & R services. These librarians are often trained to look for personal (nondocument) problems underlying the client's "presenting" query. (3) Some librarians' "reach" for resources regularly extends beyond their own agencies, as a result of performing both on-line and I & R services, whose very essence is the extension of the librarian beyond the walls of the library. (4) In time the above changes will occur not only in persons directly involved with I & R and on-line searching, but also in service staff around them, thus broadly influencing service norms and policy throughout the library.

Moreover, the profession's experience with the so-called outreach that has accompanied library service to the disadvantaged and some I & R work may have prepared it to address information needs that have not heretofore reached the reference desk. The I & R venture in some libraries has been accompanied by unprecedented levels of advertising of library services, by increased contact with the community through "community walks," by a more open information transaction with the client in order to uncover his underlying needs, and by a broadened idea of what is an acceptable information resource, including individuals, agencies, unpublished files, etc. [2]. It is quite likely that these activities, all conducted under the banner of I & R, will generate benefits for the whole library institution. There is evidence that publicity and community contact undertaken for the sake of I & R have attracted greater numbers of traditional reference questions to the library [2].

3. Library Malpractice

Any tendency to liberate the profession from reliance on published documents may find a counterforce in the growing possibility of library malpractice suits. While such fear of redress for wrong or misleading information is not widespread in the profession today, it could affect the nature of service should it become so. It is conceivable that librarians would be compelled to verify answers in multiple published sources in order to protect themselves from blame.

Technology

In addition to political, economic, individual, and professional factors, technology itself promises to affect the future of reference and information services. Several years ago, sociologist Anthony Downs told a conference of the American Library Association that the main force for innovation in an institution is technology, which is usually imposed on the institution from outside [24]. In recent years we have seen the dramatic effect of the computer (an outside technology) on bibliographic control in libraries (the institution), in the form of the OCLC and BALLOTS/SPIRES systems. In many libraries the work of cataloging and processing materials has undergone sweeping change: local idiosyncracies in cataloging have sometimes been abandoned in order to make full use of a cooperative system; the amount of original cataloging has been substantially reduced; and the speed of cataloging and processing materials has been greatly increased [25]. Moreover, a library which is a member of a large bibliographic network such as OCLC or BALLOTS/SPIRES can now communicate holdings information with many other libraries on a scale and at a speed never before possible [26]. Such bibliographic control systems are giving the local librarian an expanded awareness of the document resources available for answering clients' queries. They may prove to be the first significant step toward a national information network.

The same external technology, the computer, has given rise to sophisticated bibliographic control systems for the periodical and report literature. Through such commercial enterprises as Lockheed's DIALOG, Bibliographic Retrieval Services, Systems Development Corporation's ORBIT, and the New York Times Information Bank, libraries and their clients can now have on-line access to a gigantic store of bibliographic data—sometimes with abstracts attached—hitherto accessible only through many separate printed volumes. Connect time to these on-line services has been growing steadily cheaper, as have the terminals required for access. It is certain that connect time and the terminals will become even cheaper in years to come and that more and more libraries will be in a position to afford them. The implications for reference and information service should be obvious. Not only will the client be able to learn about a greater number and range of documents, but he will be able to do so more rapidly and with greater flexibility in the language and search strategy with which he approaches the files than has been the case in the past. Moreover, the ultimate product can be a computer-printed bibliography, with abstracts—or a copy of a complete document—that the client carries away with him.

While on-line bibliographic systems for monographic, periodical, and report literatures have been making inroads on public library reference and information activities, another computer-based source of information, the data bank, has had limited impact. Rich stores of data—particularly social data, such as the United States census—are, to my knowledge, largely outside the scope of information services currently provided by public libraries. Nonetheless, they do exist as an information resource with potential—albeit low—for the public library's future. Wire services like United Press International and Associated Press could be considered akin to social data bases in that they provide factual, rather than bibliographic, information. The public libraries of Washington, D.C., and Queens, New York, have used such wire services as much for public relations as for bona fide information services. Their adoption in a few public libraries over the past few years may presage some slight inclination in the profession to provide access to data banks. It is not likely, however, that any but the largest public libraries will offer services based on social data banks in the forseeable future.

Advances in various means of transmitting information have had and will have some impact on public library reference and information services. For several years information has been cablecast from the public libraries of Casper, Wyoming [27], and Reston, Virginia [28], to their respective clients. Demonstration of satellite transmission of information from libraries to remote Alaskan villages has already taken place [29]. To date these efforts have had little impact on the public library as an institution, even though impact on a given local library may have been great. Until the cost of the staff, software, and hardware associated with advanced transmission technologies (short wave, satellite, teletype, data-phone linkages, cable television, etc.) is reduced, it is not likely that they will take the lead over cheaper traditional technologies such as telephone and mail services.

Microforms have affected the reference and information function of public libraries by making available at the local level resources that would either be unaffordable or too large to house in paper form. Computer-output-microform (COM) affords the possibility of preparing multiple copies of computer-based catalogs for wide dissemination, as well as the possibility of generating specialized bibliographies on demand from a large file. As with most other technological innovations, microforms, including COM, should affect the reference function primarily by facilitating access to a larger store of documents than heretofore. Secondarily, COM can increase the library's flexibility in responding to the particular needs of the client by generating custom-made bibliographies and by reproducing documents at low cost.

The Growth of Documents

The exponential growth of documents continues to have a great impact on a profession that has adopted as a primary role the control of document resources for the public and individual good. As documents proliferate, the problems of their control and retrieval are exacerbated. Faced with a growing flood of potentially useful documents, the librarian and client find it more imperative than ever to retrieve those documents and only those documents that are useful to the client. The reference and information process which, in public libraries at least, has relied heavily on human memory becomes less reliable as both in-house and external document files grow. As a result, there is a predictable growth of aids—manual and automated, public and commercial—to assist in control and retrieval of these documents. *Current Contents*, the OATS Tearsheet Service, *Science Citation Index,* and *Social Science Citation Index* are some of the commercial aids that have prospered recently. On-line bibliographic services are a similar kind of response. Some of these services are available in large public libraries. If the growth of documents continues unabated, the growth of control and retrieval aids, either in the private or public sectors, is sure to continue.

It is likely, however, that the private sector will respond more quickly than the public sector to such opportunities. But, of course, it will respond with marketable commodities only. Aids that are needed but are not widely marketable will be left to the public sector to develop. Yet, as computer costs decrease over the years, it will become profitable for the information industry to develop and market information and informational aids that appeal to ever smaller and more specialized audiences. Private enterprise will seek and command a larger share of the information marketplace than ever.

Possible Futures for the Public Library

The most certain future that faces reference and information service in the public library is that there will be more divergence in the nature and level of service from library to library than there has been heretofore. The "glue" that binds public library to public library or professional librarian to professional librarian is the relatively weak one of voluntary professional association. Such association is manifested formally in organizations like the American Library Association and state and local associations. While these associations have frequently figured large in major decisions for the profession—especially certain large-scale decisions related to politics and economics—the key decisions that affect a given library and the services it offers will continue to be made at the local level. The current approach of the Public Library Association to the development of standards—or, rather, goals—for public libraries that are wholly derived from and evaluated against local community needs supports the assertion that the determination of service goals will be more local than ever before [30]. Accepting this assertion, plus the wide range of influences acting on public libraries, plus the great variety of service options that can be chosen, we can expect individual libraries to respond in quite different ways.

A given library's decision will continue to depend largely on local client needs, local political and economic realities, and the predispositions and strengths of the local staff—and very little on a national statement of philosophy or goal. To illustrate the divergence that will be possible in reference and information service, the following scenarios are presented. They represent the extremes of the decisions that can be made at the local level. No library that I know is close to future B, although many libraries have embarked on certain aspects of it.

Future A: book-based, traditional reference desk, augmented by periodicals and selected government documents and receiving an occasional telephone call and interlibrary loan request.

Future B: Free or mostly free on-line access to major bibliographic services and to several of the major data banks; mail, cable, and phone transmission of information to the client; strong links with other information sources and/or membership in a large centralized question-answering consortium; active ties to the community and governmental resources; coordination of a "public information utility" at the local level, to assure everyone equal access to information in a variety of forms and through a variety of channels [31]; free or mostly free computation facilities and assistance for clients' personal use; directories of local community organizations, community leaders, social services, governmental agencies, educational opportunities, entertainments, etc., maintained by the library and distributed to other service agencies in print or electronic form; "open" transactions with the client in which the library is receptive to personal as well as bibliographic needs; improved negotiation of the client's initial inquiry; an assertive answer-oriented rather than book-bound approach to service, in which the search for an answer frequently ranges far beyond the local walls; advocacy of the client's right to be informed in the face of intractable governmental bureaucracies; firm knowledge of the frequency and quality of the information service provided; awareness of competing or complementary information services available to the client group; frequent and vigorous advertising of reference and information services.

These scenarios will most likely come to pass primarily as a function of local economics. The wealthy community will tend to enjoy the strong, active service outlined in future B. The poor community will tend to continue with a traditional, rather passive, level of service. Between A and B we will see variations of every hue and tone, such as a library with the financial resources to provide the highest level of service but lacking the philosophical or managerial imperative to perform, or an impoverished library that manages to deliver rather full service by virtue of the persistence and ingenuity of its staff. It is certain that if the profession does not wage a vigorous effort to change from within—change its own institutions and critical external elements as well—it will be controlled from outside, and the public library's current position in the information marketplace will be further eroded.

REFERENCES

1. Gates, Jean Key. *Introduction to Librarianship*. New York: McGraw-Hill Book Co., 1968.
2. Childers, Thomas. *Third Year Continuation of a (Program to) Research and Design Criteria for the Implementation and Establishment of a Neighborhood Information Center in Five Public Libraries: Atlanta, Cleveland, Detroit, Houston and Queen's Borough. Final Report.* Washington, D.C.: U.S. Department of Health, Education, and Welfare, Office of Libraries and Learning Resources, 1975.
3. Vilma Wallis Interview. Philadelphia. Free Library of Philadelphia. New York Times Information Bank. April 14, 1978.
4. Baky, John. "Library Line 1974." *Connecticut Libraries* 16 (June 1974): 5–9.
5. Crowley, Terence, and Childers, Thomas. *Information Service in Public Libraries: Two Studies*. Metuchen, N.J.: Scarecrow Press, 1971.
6. Oettinger, Anthony G. *Elements of Information Resources Policy: Library and Other Information Services*. 2d ed. Cambridge, Mass.: Harvard University Press, 1976.
7. Slanker, Barbara O. "Public Libraries and the Information Industry." *Drexel Library Quarterly* 12 (January–April 1976): 139–48.
8. Bundy, Mary Lee. *Metropolitan Public Library Users*. College Park: University of Maryland, 1968.
9. Monat, William R. *The Public Library and Its Community*. Pennsylvania State Library Monograph Series, no. 7. University Park: Pennsylvania State University, 1967.
10. Palmour, Vernon E., and Bellassai, Marcia C. *To Satisfy Demand: A Study Plan for Public Library Service in Baltimore County*. Arlington, Va.: Public Institute, Center for Naval Analyses, 1977.
11. Chief Officers of State Library Agencies. *The Role of Libraries in America*. Frankfort, Ky.: Department of Library and Archives, 1976.
12. Gallup Organization, Inc. *The Use of and Attitudes toward Libraries in New Jersey*. Vol. 1, *Summary and Analysis*. Princeton, N.J.: Gallup Organization, Inc., 1976.
13. Dervin, Brenda, et al. *The Development of Strategies for Dealing with the Information Needs of Urban Residents. Phase I: Citizen Study, Final Report*. Washington, D.C.: U.S. Department of Health, Education, and Welfare, Office of Libraries and Learning Resources, 1976.
14. Warner, Edward S. *Information Needs of Urban Residents: Final Report*. Washington, D.C.: U.S. Department of Health, Education, and Welfare, Division of Library Programs, 1973.
15. Childers, Thomas. *The Information-Poor in America*. Metuchen, N.J.: Scarecrow Press, 1975.
16. Rein, Martin. "Social Service Crisis." *Transaction* 1 (May 1964): 3–6.
17. Shapiro, Joyce. "Perceptions of Academic Library Service Policies by Undergraduate Students and Library Staff Members." M.S. thesis, Drexel University, 1973.

18. Pings, C. P. "Reference Services Accountability and Measurement." *RQ* 16 (Winter 1976): 120–23.
19. Hanks, Gardner, and Schmidt, C. J. "An Alternative Model of a Profession for Librarians." *College and Research Libraries* 36 (May 1975): 175–90.
20. Childers, Thomas. "Statistics that Describe Libraries and Library Service." In *Advances in Librarianship,* edited by Melvin J. Voigt. Vol. 5. New York: Academic Press, 1975.
21. Weech, Terry. "Evaluation of Adult Reference Service." *Library Trends* 22 (January 1974): 315–32.
22. Prentiss, S. Gilbert. "Testing Reference and ILL Performance by Stimulating the Library-User Transaction." *Newsletter on Library Research* 17 (September 1976): 6–14.
23. Lynch, Mary Jo. "Reference Interviews in Public Libraries." Ph.D. dissertation, Rutgers University, 1977.
24. Downs, Anthony. *Library Survival and the Economics of Social Change.* Phonotape. Los Angeles; CREDR Corp., 1973.
25. Krieger, Tillie, ed. "Catalogs and Catalogers: Evolution through Revolution." *Journal of Academic Librarianship* 2 (September 1976): 172–79.
26. Plotnik, Art. "OCLC—for You—and Me?" *American Libraries* 7 (May 1976): 258–67.
27. "Cable and Libraries." *Cable Libraries* 3 (February 1975): 2–3.
28. Vohl, John. *The Reston, Virginia Test of the Mitre Corporation's Interactive Television System.* McLean, Va.: Mitre Corp., 1971.
29. "Alaska Library Delivers Services by Satellite." *Cable Libraries* 2 (May 1974): 6.
30. "PLA Drafts New Public Library Mission." *Library Journal* 102 (December 1977): 2460–61.
31. Parker, Edwin B., and Dunn, Donald A. "Information Technology: Its Social Potential." *Science* 176 (June 30, 1972): 1392–99.

EDUCATIONAL, CULTURAL, AND RECREATIONAL SERVICES OF THE PUBLIC LIBRARY FOR ADULTS

Mary Jo Lynch

No one would deny that the public library has educational and recreational functions, the two functions specified in the assigned title for this paper. The words "education" and "recreation" will be found in almost anyone's definition of the public library. What the words mean, however, differs from person to person; how they are interpreted by libraries differs from place to place. This ambiguity is one of the exciting challenges of dealing with public libraries. It makes it difficult, however, to talk in a meaningful way about their educational and recreational functions. Boyd Rayward struggled with this problem while planning the conference; we talked on several occasions about what to call this paper and what it should cover. As I prepared the manuscript, I began to wonder why we had left out the word "cultural," since cultural functions are so closely related to the other two. So I decided to put it in.

Definitions

Adding that word does not make the topic of this paper any clearer, however, and dictionary definitions do not help very much. Webster would define educational functions as those related to the "discipline of mind or character through study or instruction"; cultural functions as those related to "the enlightenment and refinement of taste acquired by intellectual and aesthetic training"; and recreational functions as those related to "the refreshment of strength and spirits after toil." But those first two definitions need broadening if they are to be useful here, and the third also needs comment.

Discipline of mind is part of education but so also is the joy of understanding something which was previously puzzling or overlooked entirely. The noncompulsory and nonjudgmental nature of the public library's role in education would seem to encourage an emphasis on the latter.

Refined taste is one meaning of culture, but there are other meanings of the word which may be more important to a public library. A culture may be thought of as a particular form or stage of civilization, and the public library can play an important role in a pluralistic society by facilitating the understanding of various cultures. Another way of looking at culture is found in a recent report from Great Britain describing *Public Libraries and Cultural Activities*. This report speaks of public library cultural services as those which "widen the horizons of the mind, and quicken understanding" [1, p. 12]. Another perspective comes from scholars like Gordon Stevenson, who suggested recently that the public library must seriously consider its relationship to what is known as "popular culture" [2]. Many would characterize the diverse activities covered by that phrase as not culture at all but merely entertainment. However, it is popular, and so are public libraries. The problem here seems to be a modern version of the classic debate between public needs and public wants.

Recreation is closely linked to popular culture if we understand the latter as embracing the things people do when they are not working. People sometimes dismiss the public library by saying that it is a recreational institution and thereby implying that it is frivolous or unnecessary. But medical experts tell us that recreation is absolutely essential to the mental health of human beings. Why then are some librarians embarrassed when the public library is called recreational?

The three concepts—educational, cultural, and recreational—taken together and broadly conceived describe the public library functions sometimes known as "adult services" [3]. It is perhaps a false dichotomy to separate these adult services from reference or information services, and in some libraries the latter are included in the responsibilities of an adult services department. Both the educational, cultural, and recreational functions of the public library and the library's reference and information services are based on that elusive commodity, information. Often the same people are involved both as librarians and as clients, and many contacts between the library and a particular client are multidimensional.[1]

One indication of the difficulty in conceptualizing these services as separate is the quiet but constant debate within the American Library Association as to whether the interests of librarians who deal directly with the adult public should be represented by two divisions of the

---

1. Patrick Wilson's *Public Knowledge and Private Ignorance*, which came to my attention too late to be considered fully in this paper, makes an interesting distinction between "the library as a source of information useful in decision making" and "the library as a source of what is simply of interest [4, p. 126]. Wilson's book deals almost exclusively with the former, though he admits that the case for the importance of libraries may rest "on the intrinsic value of the satisfaction of interests . . ." [4, p. 126]. Wilson's distinction may be useful in separating reference and information services from other adult services.

association or by one. For years there were two, the Reference Services Division and the Adult Services Division. Since 1972 there is one, the Reference and Adult Services Division, but not everyone is comfortable with this arrangement. Some adult services librarians feel that their interests are neglected by the division in favor of the interests of reference librarians.

The meaning of the word "adult" may be the only thing that is clear about what is done by a librarian or library department labeled "adult services." Eighteen seems to be commonly accepted as the age at which a person becomes an adult, though I expect Mary Kay Chelton may have some comments to make on that assertion. In any case, public library service to persons over eighteen is the focus of this paper.

Categories of Service

Some would say that all library service to persons in this age group are adult services. Others would limit the phrase to cover the educational, cultural, and recreational services of a public library which are not reference or information services. What, then, are these services? I have identified eight broad categories and will comment here both on the present status of each one and on what may happen in the future.

1. A Circulating Collection
There are some services which the public library provides just by being there. First of all, a public library provides a circulating collection of materials containing information. Someone who is not a librarian might think that last phrase unnecessarily complex. To many people a public library is a collection of books which circulate. Some are aware that a library circulates other materials and offers other services, but most people think of a public library as a place from which one takes out books. In the recent Gallup survey on "The Role of Libraries in America," the library service named most frequently by those who use libraries, as well as by those who do not, was "book loans" [5, p. 50]. Many other studies could be cited to support that finding. It is hard to see how this service would not continue in the future. It seems likely, however, that public libraries will need to expand their efforts to acquire, organize, and lend material other than books. I am referring here to other materials which convey information rather than to materials such as tools and plants which are circulated by some public libraries but which seem unlikely to be incorporated into a significant number of circulating collections.

Librarians have been accused of a "functional fixedness" which makes them largely book lenders. If that is overcome (and it has been in many cases), the problem is not therefore solved; it is merely changed. Book selection has always been a challenge for a very simple reason: The volume of material available far exceeds an individual library's ability to pay. Enlarging the scope of what is collected, however, will only make selection more difficult. Even the elegant formulas proposed by Newhouse and Alexander in their economic analysis of the Beverly Hills (California) Public Library [6] will not save librarians from hard decisions.

2. *A Noncirculating Collection*

The public library also provides materials which do not circulate either because they are too heavily used by many people or too easily damaged to be allowed to leave the premises. This also is likely to continue. It might even expand if libraries find that the heavy demand for some materials coupled with higher costs and lower budgets forces them to restrict more materials to use within the library building.

3. *Space and Equipment*

A library provides space and equipment for using library materials or for educational, cultural, and recreational activities. Reading areas, listening and viewing equipment, and meeting rooms are all part of this category, which is sometimes overlooked when public libraries list their services to the public. It will certainly grow in importance if libraries expand their collection of nonbook materials, many of which cannot be used unless special equipment is available. The lending of this equipment itself is a related service, one which some libraries are now offering as they expand the types of material in the circulating collection.

Since people use the noncirculating collection and most space and equipment within a particular building, librarians need to be very aware of the library as an environment which affects the physical and psychological comfort of people who use it. Lack of funds is not the only reason why libraries are often uninviting places; lack of imagination may be a more cogent reason in some cases. Attention to such things as sign systems, lighting, arrangement of furniture, hours, attitudes, and behavior of staff is important. Librarians can easily become accustomed to seeing the library from only one point of view—that of the person who works in a place daily. It may look different to occasional users, even to those who come often. In the future, this point of view will need more consideration.

4. *Access to Other Collections*

Another important service of the public library is to provide access to materials not in the local collection but available through a system or network. In some places this is accepted and expected, but in many communities the existence of local connections to other collections is not commonly known to users of the public library. Too often I have realized that a nonlibrarian friend was amazed when I pointed out that his or her public library would certainly be able to get, on interlibrary loan, material it did not have. Resource sharing is almost a tired phrase in the library community today. The challenge of the future is not only to make it work but also, and especially in public libraries, to let users know it exists.

5. *Delivery of Materials*
A fifth service, and one which is more familiar to the public than access to other collections, is the delivery of library materials to persons who do not use the library directly for any one of a number of reasons. Bookmobile service, books-by-mail programs, and service to the homebound, to hospitals, and to prisons are examples of this type of activity.

In a society which is becoming more and more sensitive to the needs and rights of people who are restricted or handicapped in any way, this kind of service must surely grow. Years ago, C. Walter Stone pointed out that the library is not a place but a function [7]. This idea might well inform our thinking about all aspects of library service, but it seems most relevant here. How can we expand the public library function into the lives of people who do not come to the place? Modern technology offers many anwers to that question. For example, the multiple possibilities of cable television come immediately to mind. It seems essential for the future that the public library community continue to develop expertise in the production and delivery of cable television programs and skill in handling the political aspects of cable TV.

6. *Guidance for Users*
The sixth adult service—guidance to individuals using the library— might be traced back to 1876, when Samuel Greene spoke of "The Desireableness of Establishing Personal Intercourse and Relations be- tween Librarians and Readers in Popular Libraries" [8]. From the ideas in this speech, both reference service and what was once known as readers' advisory work developed. Reference service has become infor- mation service in many places, and the readers' advisor has all but disappeared. For one thing, we recognize that not all people who use library materials are readers; some may be viewers or listeners. For another, many librarians see their role as much broader than dealing solely with library materials. They link library users with many sources of information, some of them outside the library and some of them unrecorded.

Readers' advisors do still exist, but what is more often talked about today among librarians who give guidance to individuals in public libraries is the work of a "learners' advisor." Whether or not that specific title is used, what such people do is to help individual adults learn what they want to learn with or without the involvement of library materials. This help may range from assisting the individual in selecting an appropriate course at the local community college to assisting him or her in planning an independent reading program for the next six months. The potential need for such guidance seems evident at a time when more and more adults are involved in serious and sustained efforts to learn either through formal educational programs or on their own. Material in the *Bulletin* from the National Center for Educational Brokering suggests that there are numerous opportunities for professionals who wish to help other adults plan their learning. The February 1978 issue, for example, reported on a survey of organizations which offer special information and advisory services to adult learners. One hundred twenty-four sponsors of such services were identified; forty-two were public libraries [9, p. 1].

That healthy statistic may be one result of the Adult Independent Learner project sponsored a few years ago by the College Entrance Examination Board [10]. For that project, a number of public libraries participated in a carefully planned and evaluated program of assisting adults with their learning needs. Library staff were given special preparation for this work, and careful records were kept of all activity. The Adult Independent Learner project may be the most dramatic evidence of a new direction in public library service, but a concern for the adult independent learner is not limited to the few institutions which took part in that project. Many public libraries are actively involved in the learning activities of adults. The recent formation of the Alternative Education Programs Section within the Public Library Association (PLA) is one indication of this interest, as is the decision, by the PLA Board of Directors, to consider "The Public Library as Alternative Education Agency" as one area of public library concern which will be a priority for PLA in the next few years [11].

This interest in the learning of adults is nothing new for public librarians. For decades the public library has been involved in adult education, but something is different today. Monroe [12] recently described four positions on a spectrum of ways in which the public library might be involved in adult learning. The range is from simply providing materials, to collaborating with formal educational institutions, to functioning as an independent community learning center, to sponsoring problem-centered task forces. The first two of these possibilities were important in the past; the excitement today is with the third form of involvement: the library as an independent community learning center. The fourth, sponsoring problem-centered task forces,[2] is an approach which has not been tried in many places that I know of, though it is an interesting idea to consider for the future.

The library as an independent community learning center is a model which makes a great deal of sense for the future in the face of evidence that many adults prefer to study and learn at their own pace, employing their own style of learning. The person who has accumulated much of that evidence is Allen Tough, professor in the Department of Adult Education of the Ontario Institute for Studies in Education [13, 14]. For his purposes, Tough defines a learning project as "a highly deliberate effort to gain and retain certain definite knowledge and skill, or to change in some way. To be included, a series of related learning sessions (episodes in which the person's primary intention was to learn) must add up to at least seven hours" [14, p. 2]. Several studies show that the typical project requires 100 hours, and the typical adult conducts five of them each year [14, p. 5]. Some of these projects involve instructors and classes, but over 70 percent are self-planned, and others rely on friends and peer groups [14, p. 6]. Patrick Penland reports similar findings in his just completed study of *Individual Self-Planned Learning in America* [15]. Penland also found that only 17.1 percent of the learners used libraries on a regular basis [15, p. 50]. It may be that others really did not need the public library, but perhaps they simply did not think that the library could do anything for them. One would assume that persons with self-initiated learning projects would gravitate to the public library. If they do not, it would behoove us to find out why not.

A related challenge to public libraries came earlier in the 1973 report of the Commission on Non-Traditional Study entitled *Diversity by Design* [16]. Recommendation 31 of that report reads: "The public library should be strengthened to become a far more powerful instrument for non-traditional education than is now the case" [16, p. 82]. The commission recognized that "public libraries have too long been re-garded as passive conveyers of information or recreation, available when needed, but not playing, or expected to play, active roles in the educational process. Their vast capabilities have often been ignored" [16, p. 83].

The commission may have suggested one reason why this is the case when they noted that the public library is perceived as a passive institution. Some would say that this is just fine as long as libraries are

---

2. Monroe suggests that such a task force might consider "the formulation of government policy, the development of new industrial activity in the community, breaking the barriers of racism in schools or churches, or the creation of new roles for the retired adult . . ." [12, p. 57].

excellent passive institutions. But in our society to be passive is to be passé. Some public libraries are passive and perhaps always will be. But many are very active, and still the image of passivity persists. To combat this image, in the future, individual public libraries and the public library community in general need to become much more skilled in using the many tools available to specialists in advertising and marketing and public relations. Some librarians scorn such practices; perhaps we can no longer afford to do so.

In the preceding paragraphs, we have been speaking about guidance service to adults who are involved in learning activities beyond the basic level. But public libraries also have a role in assisting individuals who are not yet ready for these activities. Literacy has been and will be a natural concern of public libraries, for here the library is not only providing a much needed service but is also developing future users of other services. What a particular public library will do about literacy depends partly upon what else is being done in the community. The American Library Association, with funds from the Office of Education, recently sponsored the publication of *Literacy and the Nation's Libraries* [17], a manual which will help librarians understand the problem of illiteracy, work with other agencies to combat it, and plan their own activities. Practitioners interested in this area have formed a task force on "Basic Education and Literacy" within the Alternative Education Programs Section of the PLA. That section also has a "Task Force on Visual Literacy and Audiovisual Communications" which might provide a partial answer to Wes Doak's complaint that library literacy programs are "elitist in concept and tunnelvisioned in scope" [18, p. 8] because of their emphasis on print literacy.

7. *Programs for the Public*

Library efforts in the area of literacy may be directed toward either individuals or groups. They serve as a link, then, to a seventh adult service—programming for groups. To some people, this is what is meant by "adult services." In the context of this paper, a program is a public event planned by library staff as an addition to the educational, cultural, and recreational life of the community. The many possibilities were enumerated well by Peggy O'Donnell and Patsy Read in the booklet on *Planning Library Programs* [19] which they prepared for "The Southwestern Mosaic: Living in a Land of Extremes," a project of the Southwestern Library Association funded through a grant from the National Endowment for the Humanities. A chart of possible program formats lists the cost, special features, advantages, and possible limitations of each; but for our purposes here, we will consider just the list of formats: film; lecture; dramatic reading; videotape; panel, debate, symposium; projects, field trips; live dance or music; crafts and other demonstrations; exhibits; book discussion groups; "buzz" groups; group interview; role play [19, p. 22–24]. We might add "classes" to this list, although it may be covered in one of the other categories. Some of these formats may not be commonly found in libraries, but many of them have been used by libraries for a long time. Libraries are sponsoring such programs today—we read about them constantly in the news section of *Library Journal*—but it is hard to get a clear picture of what is happening nationally. The best thing we have by way of a recent survey is a 1970 study of the state of Indiana, where we know, for example, that 82 percent of the central libraries serving populations of over 30,000 sponsor recreational and cultural programs [20, p. 219].

If that level of activity is occurring nationally, one wonders why this kind of library service is not considered separately in the draft, *Library Statistical Data Base*, prepared by the National Center for Higher Education Management Systems [21]. The preliminary report of this project provides an outline of a management information system for public and academic libraries by describing methods for counting common activities. The only place public programs are counted is in the data collection form on "Information Service Activity Level," where such activities as "lectures, library tours, book reviews and discussion" are categorized under the heading "Group Transactions about the Library or Library Resources" [21, p. 226]. Perhaps public programs do not happen often enough to be counted separately despite the notices in the library press.

Another possibility is that programs are not conceived of as services in their own right but as part of a library's public relations effort. The Public Relations Section of the ALA's Library Administration Division evidently does think of programs in that way; the section has just published an attractive brochure on "Producing Library-sponsored Programs and Special Events."

The importance of programs for the adult public is a controversial issue in the public library community since some libraries question the value of such activities. Baltimore County Public Library, for example, recently decided, at the end of a thorough planning process, that if the budget were cut programming for adults would be dropped. The report notes that "response to adult programming has been meager" and "the potential and effectiveness of the library program as a group information transaction and as a stimulus to materials circulation have never been thoroughly examined in the system . . ." [22, p. 37]. There is little substantive literature and practically no research on this topic. In an introduction to one of the few monographs on the subject of library programs [23], John Robotham and Lydia LaFleur discuss the reasons for sponsoring them. The most traditional is connected with public relations. Programs are offered "to lure people into the library" [23, p. vii].

Robotham and LaFleur offer other reasons. For one thing, programs "are extensions of the material on library shelves" [23, p. viii]. Also, people learn in different ways: "A macrame demonstration or a film on the population explosion might be more meaningful to some people than reading about those subjects and we, as librarians, must learn to use any medium to achieve our goals" [23, p. viii]. But what are our goals? One could argue that, since other agencies in the community are set up to do things which extend the material on library shelves and to help people learn in different ways, a public library should not spend its limited time and money on programs. This is the view implied by Goldhor and Wheeler in their classic text on public library administration [24] and vigorously expressed more recently by D. W. Davies [25]. But I wonder if it is appropriate for today and for the future.

If public libraries are to be dynamic institutions, at the center of the educational, cultural, and recreational life of a community, public programs seem to be appropriate not just as public relations efforts but because of what they do to enrich the lives of individuals. Robotham and LaFleur suggest that this may be especially important in places where "little or nothing of a cultural nature is being offered to the general public" [23, p. viii]. The National Endowment for the Humanities has indicated a willingness to support library programs, at least those which involve the humanities. The individual public library will have to decide whether library programming for adults is or could be important to the community served. This is not an easy decision since it involves the fundamental purpose of a public library. I suspect that in the future, as in the present, individual libraries will come to different conclusions about this seventh adult service.

8. *Support for Groups*

Related to a library's work in sponsoring its own programs is the supportive service which a library can offer to other groups. This is not a controversial service, perhaps because it is supportive rather than entrepreneurial. It might involve anything from providing meeting room space to maintaining a clearing house on potential speakers to sponsoring workshops on planning and producing programs. This is another adult service which might well expand in the future as Americans continue in their propensity to form associations.

Conclusion

Five years ago Zweizig's dissertation [26] noted that we have very little empirical evidence to demonstrate the role that the public library plays in the lives of adults. Because we still know so little about this role in the past or in the present, predictions about the future may be way off the mark. But we must make them nonetheless. Many believe that future prospects for the public library are not good, but I cannot accept that verdict. Study after study shows that public libraries already have the good will of a majority of the public. What we need to do now is to find ways of maximizing the perceived impact of the public library on the life of a community so that when funds are divided among competing departments of a government the library gets its fair share. This will not be easy since some governmental services—fire protection and garbage collection, for example—are obviously more necessary to the quality of life than library service. Or are they?

In the seventh volume of *Advances in Librarianship,* Zweizig and Dervin observe that in the past we liked to prove the library's value by counting circulation of materials whereas today we are more likely to count the number of users. They suggest that neither is really useful: "Although circulation and library use themselves have meaning for librarians, as such neither measure has meaning for the user or the client. The real questions are, 'Why did someone use the library? What does the person find useful that a library might be able to provide?' The important question then is not library use, not library users, but library *uses.* It is these 'uses,' these 'utilities' around which libraries can plan programs and can measure effectiveness" [27, p. 251]. We need to know a lot more about library uses before we can decide what role the educational, cultural, and recreational functions of the public library for adults described in this paper will play in establishing the public library at the center of the life of a community.

REFERENCES

1. Library Advisory Council (England) and Library Advisory Council (Wales). *Public Libraries and Cultural Activities.* Department of Education and Science, Library Information Series, no. 4. London: HMSO, 1975.
2. Stevenson, Gordon. "Popular Culture and the Public Library." In *Advances in Librarianship,* edited by Melvin Voigt. Vol. 7. New York: Academic Press, 1977.
3. Hunter, Della L. "Who, What, Where, How About Adult Services." *Southeastern Librarian* 24 (Spring 1974): 32–34.
4. Wilson, Patrick. *Public Knowledge and Private Ignorance: Toward a Library and Information Policy.* Westport, Conn.: Greenwood Press, 1977.
5. Chief Officers of State Library Agencies. *The Role of Libraries in America.* Frankfort, Ky.: Kentucky Department of Libraries and Archives, 1976.
6. Newhouse, Joseph P., and Alexander, Arthur J. *An Economic Analysis of Public Library Services.* Lexington, Mass.: Lexington Books, 1972.
7. Stone, C. Walter. "The Library Function Redefined." *Library Trends* 16 (October 1967): 181–96.
8. Greene, Samuel S. "Personal Relations between Librarians and Readers." *Library Journal* 1 (October 1876): 74–81. The longer title was used for the original reading of the paper at the American Library Association Conference.

9. "The Spread of the Brokering Idea." *Bulletin* (National Center for Educational Brokering) 3 (February 1978): 1–2.

10. Mavor, Anne S.; Toro, Jose Orlando; and DeProspo, Ernest R. "An Overview of the National Adult Independent Learning Project." *RQ* 15 (Summer 1976): 293–308.

11. "New Directions for PLA." *PLA Newsletter* 16 (Summer 1977): 1–3.

12. Monroe, Margaret E. "A Conceptual Framework for the Public Library as a Community Learning Center for Independent Study." *Library Quarterly* 46 (January 1976): 54–61.

13. Tough, Allen. *The Adult's Learning Projects.* Toronto: Ontario Institute for Studies in Education, 1971.

14. Tough, Allen. "Major Learning Efforts: Recent Research and Future Directions." Mimeographed, 1977. Available from the author, Department of Adult Education, Ontario Institute for Studies in Education.

15. Penland, Patrick R. *Individual Self-Planned Learning in America.* Pittsburgh: University of Pittsburgh, 1978.

16. Commission on Non-Traditional Study. *Diversity by Design.* San Francisco: Jossey-Bass, Inc., 1973.

17. Lyman, Helen H. *Literacy and the Nation's Libraries.* Chicago: American Library Association, 1977.

18. Doak, Wes. "Libraries and Literacy: Match or Mismatch?" In *Libraries and Literacy: The Problem of Illiteracy in the United States and What Libraries Can Do about It.* Proceedings of a workshop held at the San Francisco Public Library, September 21–22, 1973. San Francisco: Bay Area Reference Center, 1977.

19. O'Donnell, Peggy, and Read, Patsy. *Planning Library Programs.* Dallas: Southwestern Library Association, 1977.

20. Olson, Edwin E. *Survey of User Service Policies in Indiana Libraries and Information Centers.* Indiana Library Studies, report no. 10. Bloomington: Indiana State Library, 1970.

21. National Center for Higher Education Management Systems (NCHEMS). *Library Statistical Data Base: Formats and Definitions.* Working document for field review. Denver–Boulder, Colo.: National Center for Higher Education Management Systems, 1977.

22. Palmour, Vernon E., and Bellassai, Marcia C. *To Satisfy Demand: A Study Plan for Public Library Service in Baltimore County.* Arlington, Va.: Center for Naval Analysis, Public Research Institute, 1977.

23. Robotham, John S., and Lydia LaFleur. *Library Programs: How to Select, Plan and Produce Them.* Metuchen, N.J.: Scarecrow Press, 1976.

24. Goldhor, Herbert, and Wheeler, Joseph. *Practical Administration of Public Libraries.* New York: Harper & Row, 1962.

25. Davies, D. W. *Public Libraries as Culture and Social Centers.* Metuchen, N.J.: Scarecrow Press, 1974.

26. Zweizig, Douglas L. "Predicting Amount of Library Use: An Empirical Study of the Role of the Public Library." Ph.D. dissertation, Syracuse University, 1973.

27. Zweizig, Douglas L., and Dervin, Brenda. "Public Library Use, Users, Uses: Advances in Knowledge of the Characteristics and Needs of the Adult Clientele of American Public Libraries." In Voigt (ed.), [2].

EDUCATIONAL AND RECREATIONAL SERVICES OF THE PUBLIC LIBRARY FOR YOUNG ADULTS

Mary K. Chelton

The Young Adult Services Concept

Young adult (YA) services as a specialty concept in the public library emerged in the 1920s as a way to bridge the gap for early adolescents between the smaller, more personalized, and protected children's rooms and the "open ranges of the adult department" [1, p. 348]. In the New York Public Library and in the Cleveland Public Library, YA services took the form of separate rooms and collections and was conceived as an extension of children's services. In the Enoch Pratt Free Library in Baltimore, the service included a trained readers' advisor with a few introductory shelves selected for young adults. Both the readers' advisor and the shelves were physically located in the adult Popular Library.

Many libraries took more interest in the facilities and location of the separate YA rooms than in adequately trained personnel, and the resulting lack of service provided in these rooms led them to be given up as failures, even though "the need for an informed, sympathetic librarian who was trained to recognize and to respond to the needs of adolescents persisted in every department of the library" [1, p. 349]. The arguments over the location of the collection, rather than over the quality of the staff, continue to this day.

Since YA services were initially seen as a transition from children's services, and since society then definitely regarded adolescents as children, it took many years for public librarians to see that YA services, conceptually, should more logically be aligned with adult services [2, p. 3]. Some schizophrenia continues, however, because the more personalized nature of the delivery of YA services still has more in common with children's services than with adult services, even though the most interesting materials for young adults are drawn from adult sources and parallel adult interests.

While technically YA service is a specialty, with strong roots in the traditional readers' advisory function of public libraries, the specialized nature of such services does not mean that the YA librarian should not also be a generalist. YA librarians are most accurately described as library-based advocates and interpreters for adolescents. The YA services draw on all the resources of the library and the community, for , in addition to being readers' advisors, good YA librarians must also make the library a dynamic place for adolescents to be by programming activities based on their interests and talents. The unique offering of the YA service lies in its creative ability to make the library, the young adults, and the many "communities" in which each reside more understandable to each other.

YA services are humanistic rather than technical in orientation. It is no accident that they have attracted some of the most charismatic and idealistic librarians, "who have produced some of the most imaginative and responsive programs in the modern public library" [1, p. 350]. In a profession often characterized by ambivalence toward people and by affection for "things," YA librarians are outstanding in the requirement that they be consistently people centered, even when their "people" are the most difficult constituency facing the public library today.

Contemporary Adolescents

If YA services defy easy categorization, how much more difficult is the problem of defining the young adults themselves! The only consistent characteristic of adolescence is variability, a characteristic which absolutely demands an open-ended, flexible attitude on the part of any person or institution hoping to serve such a diverse group of people. There is nothing homogeneous about adolescents, and the simultaneous juggling of chronological, social, legal, academic, biological, emotional, and intellectual ages within the same person makes such a person very difficult to categorize for ready delivery of service. "Early adolescence is a time of growth second only to infancy in velocity" [3, p. v].

The most obvious component of adolescence is the acceleration of biological growth which occurs, usually before emotional development starts. In the United States, the onset of the pubertal growth spurt which heralds adolescence occurs during the tenth year for girls and during the eleventh year for boys [4, p. 5]. The onset of this growth spurt has also been starting approximately four months earlier each decade, a trend about which there is much controversy among biological researchers—and much denial on the part of institutions trying to serve adolescents [3, p. 27].

Because the growth spurt begins at the same time in two individuals does not mean that it will be completed by both of them at the same time. In some cases, one individual may complete the process before another has started it—and both may be the same age and in the same grade. A frame of reference for services to adolescents based on chronological age, therefore, may be not only inaccurate, but dysfunctional [3, p. 28].

The marked variability of adolescent development is important for librarians to recognize, not only because of the problem of definition it poses, but also because of the anxieties which it produces in the adolescents themselves. "An adolescent with delayed development is likely to have considerable difficulty in securing a sense of self-esteem, and may be inherently unsure of his biological integrity" [4, p. 6]. Such anxieties make adolescents exceptionally vulnerable psychologically and occasionally lead to unpredictable behavior.

Consider the frustration that may arise in a young person at the upper or lower end of the normal range when there are marked discrepancies between chronological age and physical appearance. How hard it is for us to accord a 16-year-old who appears to be only 12 or 13 the full degree of independence, self-determination, and decision-making to which he or she is entitled. To a substantial measure one finds such youths frequently responding to these external expectations—and possibly to inner biological cues, or lack thereof, as well—by functioning at a more immature level than they might were puberty more advanced. [4, pp. 6–7]

In addition to the other physiological changes so pronounced in adolescence, there is the experience of physical sexual maturity at the same time that there is a withdrawal of and from adult benevolent protection. The adolescent newly assesses the world in relationship to his or her more sexually mature self. Such consciousness of self in interaction with others, usually peers, is often mistaken for narcissistic conformity by adults. In reality, this adolescent experience of self in relation to others is what helps the adolescent grow and move forward from the family (or societal) protection of childhood into the interdependence of human society [5, pp. 8–9].

Adults find it difficult to understand in retrospect the degree of loneliness and insecurity most adolescents experience during this process of social and emotional growth, although these feelings are a constant theme in the personal writings of adolescents. Even when seen in potentially troublesome groups by adults, the individual group members may be feeling completely alone or different somehow, and peers provide them with a system of emotional support. One of the most significant contemporary cinematic renderings of this feeling is the film *Saturday Night Fever*, and this explains, in part, the film's appeal to adolescents.

Adolescence is a time of experimentation, as adult limits are tested and childhood values are measured and revised according to new perceptions of the world. "The experimentation necessary to adolescents usually includes a feeling of *risk*. It is their way of learning about their own and the surrounding reality" [5, p. 10]. Enormous mood swings and ambivalence are characteristic of adolescents because moving from dependence to interdependence creates all kinds of tensions and conflicts. "Seeing parents as mere humans with frailties can be terrifying after having depended on them as 'all-wise' " [5, p. 11].

Besides the physiological and emotional changes characteristic of adolescence in all cultures, American adolescents face a prolonged economic dependence because of society's educational and vocational requirements. There is little adult commitment to service structures designed for the non-school-related needs of adolescents. Making school the primary "place" for adolescents in our culture has in essence segregated them from the larger adult world. Opportunities and incentives for contact between adolescents and people older and younger than themselves are decreased.

Because of this economic and educational segregation by adults, adolescence is artificially prolonged and made into a special kind of "youth culture" by those forced into it. Deprived of psychic support from persons of other ages, subordinate and powerless in relation to adults, and outsiders to our dominant social institutions, many adolescents become reluctant to leave their youth culture after having been forced to create it. Assimilation into the dominant adult culture from which they have been segregated becomes a crisis for them, especially in relation to employment.

Impediments to Young Adult Services

Adequate Personnel

Despite the valiant efforts of a small group of dedicated practitioners around the country, and despite the marginal survival of ALA's Young Adult Services Division (YASD) under the new dues structure of the association, YA services continue to be an "endangered species" in terms of personnel. A simple count of the full-time-equivalent professionals dedicated to YA services in the public library at all levels is revealing of the specialty's status. There are only five and one-half state-level YA specialists [6]. In 468 public library systems serving populations of 100,000 or more, there are only 121½ YA coordinators or paid consultants [7]. Within states like New York, with twenty-two public library systems and a long history of public library service before systems, there are only eight and one-half system-level YA specialists [8].

At the local library level, YA services are usually the part-time responsibility of an entry-level librarian who is part of another department or function such as, for example, children's services or adult reference services. To advance up the general professional career ladder, these librarians usually seek promotions out of the specialty. Those who come new to YA positions or who are left behind are confronted with a specialty career ladder that is almost nonexistent. Worse still, they have to "reinvent" the YA services themselves because of the lack of leadership produced by the constant depletion of potentially expert personnel.

One myth surrounding this process is that those who are promoted out of YA services are then able to support the specialty from their new, better-paid positions of authority. I have yet to see any research substantiating this supposition, nor is there anything in my own experience which would give credence to it.

Training
While library schools are consistently found wanting in some form or another, or are treated as scapegoats for our professional inadequacies, nowhere are they more vociferously damned than by YA librarians working in the public libraries.

First of all, the number of library schools with a YA services course as opposed to, or in addition to, a YA literature course is miniscule. Any YA librarian can tell any educator that reading a "magic list" of titles does not provide adequate preparation for the realities of YA services today. A recent study by Mary Kingsbury to determine the priorities of YA practitioners versus those of library educators revealed that the practitioners "place a higher priority on the two areas of adolescent problems and programming than do the educators" [9]. She also points out that, while YA librarians constantly lament their lack of training in adolescent development, there is little commitment on the part of educators to meeting this need.

Whatever YA courses do exist in library schools are usually electives within the curriculum except for those students who wish to be certified as school media specialists. Sometimes, such courses are actually taught in schools of education in a cooperative arrangement with the library school. In both places the courses are more often taught by a school rather than a public library specialist. By this means the library schools help reinforce society's segregation of educational services for adolescents into schools and offer little chance for library school students to explore the potential services public libraries might offer young adults.

Worse still is the tendency in library schools to include YA literature or services as part of a course on children's work and taught by children's specialists. Such an arrangement perpetuates the professional stereotype of YA services as an extension of or appendage to children's services and ill prepares students for the realities of adolescent interests and behavior. As the most significant examination of adolescence in a decade, *Growing Up Forgotten*, points out, " . . . American society functions on the basis of several widespread myths about adolescents, who they are and how they are best served. . . . A second myth is that junior-high-aged adolescents are children, or at most in a transitional stage between childhood and adolescence" [3, pp. iv–v].

Because their courses in YA literature or services are electives (when they are offered), library schools graduate a great many people who get no exposure to concepts of YA service. There seems to be little attempt to integrate these concepts into the total curriculum, even though many YA materials and the special skills of YA librarians are also useful with poor adult readers or for answering general reference questions. Adult services librarians are limited by the segregation of these concepts from the entire curriculum.

I might add that the greatest intellectual freedom problems in public librarianship consistently occur in the YA services area, so graduating potential public library administrators who have had no exposure to these services is especially self-defeating. YA services concepts must be integrated into the entire library school curriculum and must not continue to be segregated in the same way in which adolescents are segregated from the majority culture. Moreover, library schools must begin to recognize that there are radical differences in philosophy between public library YA librarians and secondary school media specialists; courses should be organized accordingly.

Administrative Rigidity
If children's services can be supported in all but the smallest public libraries, we must ask why services to adolescents cannot. The easiest answer is that administrators are perpetuating the myth that adolescents are children and indeed are being served by their children's librarians. The fact that no children's librarian in the United States will comfortably buy Judy Blume's novel for adolescents, *Forever,* escapes the notice of administrators. Such administrators do not have to defend either the creation of another staff position or the intellectual freedom rights of young adults. Better yet, since children's services are generally segregated administratively from adult services, and since children's rooms keep the children separate from the "fair garden" of adult materials, unruly adolescents, by this administrative view, are kept separate too. The fact that many adolescents become nonusers of a library so organized and never return voluntarily also escapes administrative attention.

It is equally interesting to examine another administrative ploy used to keep YA positions from being established. The argument runs that specialists for such a brief age span, which only they seem to have defined, are too expensive, and that they tend to be inflexible; library generalists are what is needed, people who can do a little bit of everything. The fact is that "generalist" usually translates into "an ability to work with adult reference materials." The argument is doubly ironic since, in reality, YA specialists generally work very well with adults and would be fired if they did not, whereas the true inflexibility of most library staffs is found in adult reference departments whose grudging, fact-oriented service to adolescents is tolerated by these same administrators. A good adolescent specialist, by definition, is the most flexible librarian on any staff. The variability of adolescents demands it.

It has become a bromide to say that adolescents are the future taxpaying adult supporters of the public library. Administrators will consistently agree and just as consistently ignore the needs of this clientele by creating no structure through which to serve them. Since this seems to me to be like digging your own grave, I feel called upon to say, once again, that the young adults of today are the future adult taxpayers of tomorrow.

Research

Except for student-use studies, YA services as a research topic are consistently ignored by the library research community. *Doctoral Dissertations in Library Science* lists only three dissertations indexed under "young adult" which have been accepted by accredited library schools from 1930 to 1975 [10]. We don't even know for certain who is actually serving young adults in our public libraries.

To my knowledge, no one has ever studied the effects on services of separate versus interfiled collections for young adults, of different staffing patterns in similar libraries, or of the same materials in differing formats. No one has even examined the non-school-related motivating factors which bring adolescents into public libraries.

While much can be deduced from empirical observation on the job, this paper being a prime example, in formal research terms, YA services in the public library is missionary territory. We are operating on a combined philosophical basis of nostalgia and mythology.

Future Directions for Young Adult Services

If the inadequate staff, training, administration, and research of the past can be rectified, and if futile arguments over the definition of adolescents can be laid to rest, public library services to young adults might begin to set goals for the future.

The overall goal within which specific library objectives are determined should be "to provide adolescents with conditions for healthy development" such as those outlined by Gisela Konopka, Director of the Center for Youth Development and Research at the University of Minnesota, in a proposed national youth policy statement. Conditions for healthy development would, according to Konopka, provide young people with the following opportunities:

> to participate as citizens, as members of a household, as workers, as responsible members of society;
> to gain experience in decision making;
> to interact with peers and acquire a sense of belonging;
> to reflect on self in relation to others and to discover self by looking outward as well as inward;
> to discuss conflicting values and formulate their own value system;
> to experiment with their own identity, with relationships to other people, with ideas; to try out various roles without having to commit themselves irrevocably;
> to develop a feeling of accountability in the context of a relationship among equals;
> to cultivate a capacity to enjoy life. [5, pp. 14–15]

To meet this goal as outlined by Konopka, I propose the following four specific objectives for public librarians, in addition to eliminating the impediments to service outlined above.

1. *Restructure the physical environment of public libraries.* — Young adults need group interaction with their peers and with persons of other ages, and this need should be made an intrinsic part of any architectural planning or remodeling. Public libraries are rarely used by solitary adolescents in pursuit of a good book to read in relative silence. Adolescents come, instead, to do homework together and to meet friends, or because they are bored and facilities for them elsewhere in the community are inadequate or nonexistent. They come as truants when school becomes intolerable. They come for dope deals or to get out of the cold in the winter and the heat in the summer or to use the bathrooms. They come to harass the library staff for amusement; and, occasionally, they come as runaways to avoid an intolerable, abusive home situation. A good book is usually incidental to the primary motivation of adolescents for coming to the library, and it is time that we planned their socializing, developmental needs into our buildings instead of maintaining some sort of regulatory procedural warfare with them.

The ideal facility to allow peer group interaction with adult supervision "should be a separate, glass-enclosed area where conversations can be held and music can be played without disturbing other patrons" [2, p. 17]. Those adolescents who do prefer solitude at any particular time can then use the more individualized, quiet areas also provided. The continual architectural emphasis on single, multipurpose, study-hall-type rooms in which all patrons, regardless of age, are expected to coexist in relative silence is absurd if adolescent needs are considered.

Besides the staff who serve them, it is often the architectural atmosphere of the library which makes or breaks a service program for young adults.

2. *Involve young adults in library policy setting.* —Consideration should be given to developing adolescent membership on library boards. If this is not legally possible, then attempts to set up informal youth advisory boards should be made—and those boards used. While it is not suggested that libraries develop a professional group of adolescents who presume to speak for all their age group, opportunities which allow them to organize and run their own show must be incorporated into the library setting if we are to facilitate their experience of decision making and if we are to maximize what the library can offer them in terms of healthy development.

3. *Expand the programming role of the YA librarian.* —Two of the main advantages public libraries have for adolescents are that (a) they are voluntary in nature, and (b) they are not schools. Since formal, compulsory schooling dominates the adolescent experience in the United States, it is worthwhile to examine exactly what schools do. As stated in *Youth, Transition to Adulthood*:

Schools are the principal formal institutions of society intended to bring youth into adulthood. But schools' structures are designed wholly for self-development, particularly the acquisition of cognitive skills and of knowledge. At their best, schools equip students with cognitive and non-cognitive skills relevant to their occupational futures, with knowledge of some portion of civilization's cultural heritage, and with the taste for acquiring more such skills and knowledge. They do not provide extensive opportunity for managing one's affairs, they seldom encourage intense concentration on a single activity, and they are inappropriate settings for nearly all other objectives involving responsibilities that affect others. Insofar as these objectives are important for the transition to adulthood, and we believe they are, schools act to retard youth in this transition, by monopolizing their time for the narrow objectives schools have. [11, p. 146]

To structure public library YA services only to meet the school-related needs of adolescents is a major disservice in terms of the conditions for healthy development outlined here and by Konopka above. Public library experiences should become an alternative to school for young adults, rather than another variation on an outmoded, monopolistic theme. It is in the programming area where these experiences might best be created.

4. *Create an interdisciplinary adolescent services network.* —One of the most consistent themes in *Growing Up Forgotten*, besides the lack of training all adults responsible for services to adolescents feel, is their sense of isolation, even within their own institutions. Nearly all adults serving adolescents outside schools need an interdisciplinary supportive network

among themselves, not only to reinforce their commitment and to clarify mutual objectives, but also to influence the policy vacuum in regard to adolescents that exists at all levels of government. Starting such networks at the local level should be a major priority of YA librarians in the next decade. The liaison model developed by YASD's National Organizations Serving the Young Adult Liaison Committee and accepted by the YASD board at the 1977 annual ALA conference is based on such local relationships. The increased communication that is possible among those working with adolescents also gives us the potential of creating a major support group for assistance in combating organized censorship attacks, as well as the potential for creating an advocacy lobby for youth services.

As the United States reaches zero population growth, a youth services lobby will be more important than ever. In public libraries, we are already seeing the declining youth population being used as yet another rationalization for initiating nothing for them or for eradicating services long in existence, if minimally supported. While many services areas and goals need serious reexamination by public librarians, ultimately the most important thing to remember in terms of YA services is that zero population growth does not equal zero young people. We should begin now to decide what we are going to do with and for the ones who will still be around.

REFERENCES

1. Fenwick, Sara Innis. "Library Service to Children and Young People." *Library Trends* 25, no. 1 (July 1976): 329–60.
2. American Library Association, Young Adult Services Division, Services Statement Development Committee. *Directions for Library Service to Young Adults.* Chicago: American Library Association, 1977.
3. Lipsitz, Joan. *Growing Up Forgotten: A Review of Research and Programs concerning Early Adolescence.* Durham: Learning Institute of North Carolina, 1975.
4. Hofmann, Adele; Becker, R. D.; and Gabriel, H. Paul. *The Hospitalized Adolescent.* New York: Free Press, 1976.
5. Konopka, Gisela. "Requirements for Healthy Development of Adolescent Youth." *Adolescence* 8, no. 31 (Fall 1973): 1–26.
6. "Directory of State Library Agencies and Related Organizations." *ASLA President's Newsletter* 8, no. 1 (January 1978): 5–26.
7. American Library Association, Children's Services Division. *Directory, Coordinators of Children's Services and of Young Adult Services in Public Library Systems Serving at Least 100,000 People.* Chicago: American Library Association, 1977.
8. University of the State of New York, State Education Department, Library Development. *Directory of New York State Public Library Systems.* Albany, N.Y.: Library Development, 1977.
9. Kingsbury, Mary. "Educating Young Adult Librarians: Priorities of Practitioners and Educators." *Drexel Library Quarterly* 14 (January 1978): 4–18.

10. Davis, Charles H., comp. *Doctoral Dissertations in Library Science: Titles Accepted by Accredited Library Schools, 1930–1975*. Ann Arbor, Mich.: University Microfilms International, n.d.
11. **President's Science Advisory Committee, Panel on Youth.** *Youth: Transition to Adulthood*. Chicago: University of Chicago Press, 1974.

EDUCATIONAL AND RECREATIONAL SERVICES OF THE PUBLIC LIBRARY FOR CHILDREN[1]

Mae Benne

Before considering the changes in children's services over the past decade and their implications for collection development, two factors should be noted. First of all, children's librarians from the beginning have accepted John Locke's philosophy that learning for the young should be pleasurable [1, p. 115]. If pressed, most children's librarians today would have difficulty separating services and programs into discrete categories of "educational" and "recreational." A film program can appear recreational to the casual bystander and perhaps to most of the library staff as well; yet, through its pattern and execution, it may provide an experience for the participants that can only be characterized as educational. A sharp distinction between these two types of services will not be attempted in this paper.

Second, children's librarians and adult services librarians have often differed in their approach to collection development. Children's librarians traditionally have attempted to provide the best collection possible as the foundation for their service, while designing special programs to bring the child to the reading experience [2, p. 37]. In the early years of children's services, the need for quality literature focused attention on the publishers, authors, and illustrators of juvenile books. Child psychology was in its initial stages and its implications for library services unclear. The aesthetic qualities of books, rather than psychological values, tended to be stressed in selection [3, unpaged]. Adult services librarians, however, have traditionally placed more reliance on the community as the guide to collection development. The underlying assumption was that a match between the user and her or his obvious needs would result in library use.[2] Publicity was the customary means employed to bring user and materials together. In children's services, the program served as the magnet.

---

1. The author is indebted to the Council on Library Resources, Inc., for a 1976–77 fellowship to identify the role and function of the central children's library in metropolitan libraries. A significant portion of this paper draws on data obtained from this study.
2. In the selection of adult materials, the priority has shifted from one of emphasis on quality of materials to a concern for the user. This change can be observed in [4, 5, 6].

Present-day children's services and programs, considered individually and stripped of their contemporary trappings, are not of themselves vastly different from those offered in previous decades. A sampling of the literature over the period 1920–60 reveals an earlier prototype for nearly every service offered today, including some now heralded as innovative. However, in the past decade the number and variety of scheduled programs have increased, and the emphasis given various services and age groups has changed. In discussing these changes, I will deal with the following subjects: the young child and her or his parents; the elementary-school-aged child; relationships to the community; and the impact of measures of service on program priorities and the implications of these changes on collection development and staffing patterns.

The preschool story hour for children three–five years of age became widespread in the years following World War II. At that time some librarians questioned serving a group not yet able to read; others debated whether or not games and other activities included in the program could be justified as library service. Research in early childhood education over the past two decades, however, has provided a firm base on which to develop library services to the young child [7, pp. 3–10]. Moreover, the reassessment of the parent's role in the learning process currently taking place may result in more far-reaching changes in public library services.

Parents

Until recently, the children's librarian viewed the parents of the young child as potential users of library materials, either for themselves or for their children, rather than as a resource in achieving the objectives of children's services [8, p. 28]. After the child, the attention of the children's librarian usually centered on the elementary teacher, who was considered the most influential adult in the child's growth to literacy and reading. Both librarian and teacher directed considerable energy to the task of compensating for the perceived lack of intellectual stimulation and aesthetic experience in the home. It was this concept that provided the impetus for the Head Start Program and also accounted for its major shortcoming [9, p. 361]. Research has supported an idea expounded by John Amos Comenius in his *Great Didactic* over 300 years ago that the parent is the child's first teacher and needs support in performing this role [10, pp. 259–65].

Not only must the library's relationship with the parent change but also with all who share a professional or personal interest in the young child. First of all, the parent must be viewed as an ally to be supported;

second, the objectives of the service or program must be communicated to the parent if program effectiveness is to be measured; and third, special program materials and the skills of the librarian must be shared with the parent if a carry-over is expected [11, p. 56]. Some libraries have incorporated the major objectives of a program into their promotional materials; others have allowed adults to attend the children's programs or have provided the parents with a list of activities and materials used in the session with suggestions for home activities. Programs for parents in some libraries have focused on the skills and information needed to provide a stimulating environment for the child rather than on the promotion of library materials.

Commentary on the Toy

The societal changes in the past decade which have placed increasing numbers of young children in day-care facilities have encouraged a closer relationship between libraries and community agencies governing or licensing such facilities. This development, plus the growth and improvement of elementary school libraries, are reflected in the "Task Force on Children's Services Working Paper" submitted to the PLA Standards Committee in 1973 [12, pp. 26–27]. The implications of this rather revolutionary document are far reaching and have yet to be fully understood. In it, the provision of children's library services is viewed as a community responsibility, with the public library entering into an active partnership with other agencies and institutions concerned with the child. The "lady bountiful" or "welcome wagon" approach is rejected, and libraries are advised to plan with other agencies and community representatives, both children and adult, in establishing goals and developing services. This is not to imply that community agencies have been ignored in the past; but they were often seen as an audience to be served, rather than as a partner with whom to plan. With the exception of the schools, services to community groups usually appeared in last place in the listing of service objectives. Such groups were often difficult to reach and required a considerable investment of time, which was not easy to justify in terms of library use. Some library administrators approved the concept of community outreach as long as the children's librarian did not cross the street or disrupt the library's schedule.

It is in the consideration of the toy as an appropriate addition to the collection that this new relationship with community groups can be observed. In one library system, the addition of toys grew out of a working experience with other agencies serving the young child. The toy was seen as a means to increase the effectiveness of programs already in progress and to extend service to a group not presently served: the child eighteen months–three years of age placed in family day-care homes. The library staff in this system received instruction from the public school's parent education specialist in techniques of introducing toys to children and, also, in how to teach these techniques to adults. The objectives of this program were to increase the interaction of adult and child and to convey to the adult who cares for the child the importance of developing the child's verbal and intellectual abilities. The day-care mother's relationship with the library, initiated in this way, led easily into an awareness of other resources and services available through the library, while the experience gained by the library staff carried over in planning services for children and adults in other situations [13, pp. 22–28]. In assessing the long-range benefits to the library, one might discover that the experience of the children's librarian as a learner, with another agency the teacher, was of first importance. This strengthens the partnership of the library with other community agencies and, in addition, provides a valuable resource for library staff development.

In the more traditional approach to the consideration of the toy as a new material form, its place in the collection is often justified by the acknowledgment that toys are educational, are readily enjoyed by children, and provide consumer education for parents who may test before buying. Toys also gain favorable publicity for the library and serve as an aid in programming for young children. This approach, worthy as it may be, misses the opportunity to offer a more solid contribution to parent education.

It should be noted that there is not a consensus on the effectiveness of the toy as an educational resource. Some psychologists believe that toys must be matched to the child's developmental stage to be effective and that "what may be missing from our communities are not toys in libraries . . . but the cultural milieu where parents can learn of the child's need for stimulation" [14, p. 169]. Programs and services that stress child-adult interaction promise to be more effective in achieving the benefits claimed by advocates of toys.

Storytelling and the Special Program

While services to the young child have been developing an educational foundation, those for the elementary school child appear to have become more recreational in nature than in the past, especially in communities where the school library has made considerable strides in serving the educational needs of children [15, p. 3]. Unfortunately, some public libraries have interpreted a decline in children's circulation statistics to mean that school libraries are now able to meet the educational needs of children, when, in many instances, support for elementary school libraries has eroded in the past several years. In those public libraries reporting a decline in children's use, the adequacy of elementary school libraries may be less a factor in this decline than the inability of the library to adjust hours of service and staffing patterns to meet changing conditions of family life. The increase in the number of families with one parent or with both parents employed outside the home has resulted in more children being placed in custodial and educational agencies during the weekday. For many of these families, the weekend offers the most convenient time to use the public library. However, most libraries have found it difficult to increase public service hours or to offer a full range of services and programs during the weekend. Changes in teaching methods also may have affected the way children consider the services and programs offered by the library: In both the sciences [16, p. 233] and the social sciences [17, pp. 157–64], efforts have been made to involve the child in the learning process, not only as an active participant, but also as a creator of information. Libraries which offer little opportunity for the user to interact with materials may not appear to some children to be interesting places in which to spend time.

Programs, on the other hand, which offer a variety of activities or involve learning a skill appear to draw more of the older children to the library than the traditional story hour. Whether their interest in these more diverse and creative activities are reactions to the passiveness of television viewing or a preference developed through changed teaching methods, or both, is open to conjecture. It is in the effort to appeal to the widest possible audience that many libraries have incorporated a number of activities into a single program, such as a story told and a film or puppet presentation, followed by a dramatic activity, singing game, or craft inspired by the story or film [18, p. 43]. This type of program, however, requires a wide array of resources and talents, which some libraries have attempted to provide through the use of volunteers who develop program materials and assist with the more routine tasks. Volunteer talent has also been featured to provide variety and to encourage community involvement.

For some time libraries have reported that the audience for traditional story-hour programs is drawn primarily from among the children in the early elementary grades [19, p. 14] and that the numbers in attendance have also declined [20, pp. 82–83]. Some children's librarians believe that television's more sophisticated fare is the reason; others point to the reluctance of many children's librarians to invest the time needed to perfect this art when other kinds of programs draw larger numbers. However, the interest in storytelling among adults has grown. Perhaps older children might approach this traditional art with more appreciation and enjoyment if the public library were to offer to teach them the techniques of storytelling. The recent publication of a number of works dealing with storytelling will undoubtedly result in more attention being given to ways of presenting programs to contemporary audiences, both children and adults.[3]

The allocation of library resources for a special program which offers a variety of activities appears to be gaining favor in providing experiences in the library not available elsewhere in the community. Developed around a theme, such as the heritage of an ethnic group, this kind of program attracts a wide range of ages, including adults, and offers a variety of activities from which to choose: films, stories, crafts, exhibits, demonstrations by members of the community, and staff. If coordinated with an area of study in the school curriculum, it also provides an opportunity to extend learning into the community. Other special events, such as a performance by a professional drama, dance, or mime group or a talk by a visiting author which have to be supported by special grants or budgeted funds, also serve to give the library greater visibility. All of these programs draw attention in the community to the library as an important educational or cultural resource.

In determining which service should be placed in highest priority or which programs best serve the goals of the library, the children's librarian and the administrator have not always had a common understanding of objectives or community needs. One question that has always plagued the children's librarian is what determines the appropriateness of a library program. Goals often lend themselves to many interpretations. Concern has been expressed that libraries today, in an attempt to attract the child, have engaged in some rather bizarre practices for publicity purposes at the expense of other service options. Is the appearance of the police department's new helicopter on the library lawn, for example, a justifiable expenditure of library resources? Such a phenomenon could be justified as a valuable educational experience for children who seldom leave their neighborhoods. Even if it served only to give the library greater publicity, it might still be a worthwhile activity; but in that case, perhaps library departments other than the children's should be expected to share in this effort.

Measurement of Service

The measures presently used to evaluate program effectiveness often

3. Baker and Greene [21] offer a practical manual for librarians through all the planning steps: selection, preparation, and presentation; Bauer [22] focuses on media to accompany storytelling; Pellowski [23] presents a historical and theoretical approach.

determine which program will be offered. In response to pressure for more impressive attendance figures, many libraries have allocated their resources to programs which appeal to a broad spectrum of age levels. Film and puppet programs attract more participants than other types of programs. In some communities where opportunities are limited for children to enjoy the stimulation of a large audience of their peers, programs of this kind may serve a real need [24, p. 5]. However, there are other needs to be considered. The library may be the only place where a child can hear a story told, read a book at leisure, receive assistance in pursuing an interest of her or his own choosing, or be surrounded by a learning environment that makes no special demands on her or his attention.

The measurements used may also hamper the efforts of the children's librarian to enter into a cooperative relationship with the schools. If the librarian visits classrooms to tell stories or give book talks, is the effectiveness of this activity to be measured by the actual presence of children at the public library within a stated interval of time? If the result is to increase the child's interest in ideas and in the use of materials in the classroom or school library, does this further the goal of public library service?

Without clearly defined goals, it is not always easy to determine what should be measured in any particular program. In their study of the effectiveness of creative dramatics and storytelling in a library setting, Amato, Emans, and Ziegler found that neither activity appeared to have had an effect on reading achievement, but in both groups there were indications of a more positive attitude toward the library. The storytelling group took out more books and showed greater gains in developing a positive self-image, empathy, and creativity than the creative dramatic group, even though previous research had shown that creative dramatics is more effective in developing a positive self-image [25, pp. 161–62]. Is storytelling to be preferred because of book circulation? Does a positive self-image have a relationship to future library use?

In the design of individual programs, however, the linking of objectives to measurable outcomes is long overdue. Zweizig and Dervin in their study of users and uses of information suggest that a new approach to evaluation might produce more useful data than has been obtained in the past. The approach they suggest is to ask users how or if the information they obtained at the library helped [26, p. 252]. The process used for evaluation by Barass, Reitzel and Associates in their study of exemplary reading-related programs also involved the participants, including teachers and parents of young children. With some refinement, this could serve as a beginning for better measurement of program effectiveness [27, pp. 6–7].

Collections

Collections will probably continue to reflect community needs to a greater extent than in the past, partly because of the availability of a broader range of materials. Depending on the strength of school libraries, the collections for school-aged children in public libraries will stress materials for leisure use or for special interests, while the adult collection will serve as an additional educational resource for them. In some communities, however, the need for attractive, easy-to-read materials and tutoring services is critical and must be addressed by all agencies concerned with the child; this includes, of course, the public library. It seems evident that materials for the young child, on the other hand, will continue to reflect the emphasis on education, both in content and in format.

The needs of parents require consideration on a community level and by the library as a whole. Present policies governing the location and degree of duplication of materials should be examined on the basis of their effectiveness in helping parents and other child-oriented adults provide the best possible learning environment for their children. In some libraries, the best arrangement might be to designate a family area for both children and parents; in others, materials for the very young child, aged eighteen–thirty-six months, might be shelved in a separate section for the convenience of the parent. Materials may need repackaging for specific purposes. For instance, kits with a variety of forms of materials—a book, toy, recording, puppet, grouped according to a single theme and accompanied by instructions for use, would increase the effectiveness of the collection for adults working with young children.

Libraries have begun to consider games, puzzles, and other realia as items for circulation in addition to their use within the library. With the exception of the framed art print, which is challenged today by the poster in popularity, the place of realia in public library service to the school-aged child is less well established than for the young child. Continuing research in game and learning theory may be helpful in suggesting new uses for these materials in libraries for all the different age levels. In any event, the inclusion of recommended lists of these materials in selection aids for libraries serves to encourage their purchase while the annotations in the lists suggest ways in which they can be used [28, pp. 215–16].

To meet the demands for more diversified programming, storytelling collections, long a resource for librarians and other child-oriented adults, should be supplemented by additional materials. Puppets and scripts, videotapes of programs often requested by visiting classes, and materials and instructions for simple crafts to accompany programs are resources as surely as books, films, or recordings. Many of these additional materials need to be created, however, and this requires a greater commitment in the library than has been generally the case in the past to enlarged and more varied staff resources. To achieve these, a more effective balance between staff and materials in budget allocations needs to be found or changes in the deployment of existing staff must be made.

Two Critical Issues

Overall, there are two issues that must be addressed before children's educational and recreational services can be integrated into the overall services of the library or can make an impact on the community. One is the function of the children's program within the library; the other is the appropriate relationship with the community.

Interest in scheduled programming for children in the past decade has been a little short of phenomenal. Professional associations at all levels have been involved actively in the development and promotion of program materials. Any conference that offers an exchange of program ideas is assured of an audience. Unfortunately, other considerations, such as the relationship of the program to the overall services of the library or how to help those attracted by the program to make use of the resources of the library, have not received comparable attention. Children's librarians have been encouraged to develop skills in group activities and in the performing arts, which has often resulted in their giving less attention to the needs of the individual child.

The function of the program in children's services today has expanded beyond its original purpose of bringing the child to the reading experience. It has become an end in itself in much the same way as the book or other material and holds the same potential for a worthwhile experience. Considered from this point of view, budgeting for programs is as necessary to library service as for materials in the collection. Like these, however, the value of a program must be judged by its compatibility with library goals. The function of the children's library program has received little discussion in the professional literature. In observing the fate of the budget requests for resources for programs, one becomes aware that many administrators obviously have not viewed the program as an essential component of library service. Children's librarians, while aware of the support needed to provide programs, have either assumed that there is common agreement on the function of the programs or, in responding to the need to make the library more visible, have confined their attention to the programs' content and promotion.

Traditionally, children's librarians have considered the literary experience to be the most significant contribution of the library to the growth of the child. The "right book for the right child at the right time" is a worthy goal, but it may be as elusive as the dictum "to serve the whole child" embraced by our colleagues in schools of education. Bringing the child to the reading experience will undoubtedly remain as a strong pillar of children's library services, but the importance of this goal to the library may not be the same as to the child. Not all children who attend a program or use a service of the library are ready to engage in the literary experience and, indeed, may never be. But a variety of services and programs offered by the library can expose the child to the world of ideas, imagination, and creative expression. A single program, for example, can lead to a quest for information, can enrich the reading experience, or can *be* the experience. It is also an invitation to use the services of the library, and, as such, the library must consider the staff resources necessary to encourage those ready to become users. Too often, this aspect receives little consideration in program planning.

If an active partnership with community agencies is to be achieved, librarians will have to put aside, occasionally, at least, the comfortable role of teacher and adviser. Librarians have often viewed community groups with concern for children's educational and recreational needs as competitors for the child rather than as providing opportunities for co-operation in meeting children's needs more effectively. The public might be better served, for instance, if a city's recreation department offered its craft programs at the library and if the library trained story-tellers for the summer park program. For this type of relationship to evolve, the children's librarian must develop those abilities and skills that best represent the unique contribution of the library. To meet the needs of children and their parents on a community level, a different yardstick will have to be devised for measuring services from that used in the past, a yardstick that includes but goes beyond the reading experience. If we fail in this attempt, we may have to shrink the service to fit the existing measures. In so doing, we may miss the opportunity that lies before us: to write a new and exciting chapter in children's librarianship rather than a postscript to past glories.

REFERENCES

1. Locke, John. *Educational Writings*. Edited by John William Adamson. Educational Classics. London: Edward Arnold, 1912.
2. Long, Harriet G. *Rich the Treasure*. Chicago: American Library Association, 1953.
3. Brand, Barbara Elizabeth. "Influence of Higher Education on the Development of Sex-typing in Three Professions, 1870–1920." Ph.D. dissertation in progress, University of Washington.
4. McDonald, Bernice. *Library Activities in Public Libraries: A Report of a Study of Services to Adult Illiterates*. Chicago: American Library Association, 1966.

5. Public Library Association, Committee on Services to the Functionally Illiterate. *Public Library Services for the Functionally Illiterate: A Survey of Practices.* Edited by Peter Hiatt and Henry T. Drennan. Chicago: American Library Association, 1967.

6. Lyman, Helen Huguenor. *Library Materials in Service to the Adult New Reader.* Chicago: American Library Association, 1973.

7. Doan, Robert L. "Preschool Profile: Developmental Aspects of Young Children." In *Start Early for an Early Start,* edited by Ferne Johnson. Chicago: American Library Association, 1976.

8. North Carolina Central University. *Evaluation Report for Institute for Public Libraries in Service to Young Children, 1972–1973.* Durham: North Carolina Central University, 1975.

9. Strom, Robert. "Play and Family Development." *Elementary School Journal* 74 (March 1974): 359–68.

10. Comenius, John Amos. *The Great Didactic.* Translated and edited, with a biographical, historical, and critical introduction by M. W. Keatinge. London: Adam & Charles Black, 1910.

11. Tate, Binnie L., and Lange, Phil C. *The Role of the Public Library as an Alternative Force in Early Childhood Education.* Commissioned Papers Project, Teachers College, no. 3. New York: Columbia University, 1974.

12. Public Library Association. Committee on Standards. "Task Force on Children's Services Working Paper (Revised July 1973)." Community Library Services: Working Papers on Goals and Guidelines. IV. *School Library Journal* 20 (September 1973): 36–37.

13. Orr, Nancy Young. "Toys That Teach." In Johnson (ed.), [7].

14. Pilling, Marilyn, and Hayton, Greg. "Toy Lending, a Valid Public Library Service?" *Ontario Library Review* 59 (September 1975): 167–69.

15. Kingsbury, Mary. "Paper for President's Preconference, June 16, 1977." In *The Changing Role in Children's Work in Public Libraries: Issues and Answers. A Post-Conference Report on a Pre-Conference Workshop. June 16, 1977.* Detroit: Detroit Public Library, 1977.

16. McDermott, Lillian C. "Teacher Education and the Implementation of Elementary Science Curricula." In *Assessment and Development of Professionals: Theory and Practice,* edited by Preston P. LeBreton. Seattle: University of Washington, Continuing Education, 1976.

17. Jarolimek, John. "New Challenges in Social Studies Education." *Wilson Library Bulletin* 49 (October 1974): 157–64.

18. Benne, Mae. *Central Children's Library in Metropolitan Public Libraries.* Seattle: University of Washington, School of Librarianship, 1977.

19. Kane, Alice. "Starting the Story Hour." *Ontario Library Review* 54 (March 1970): 13–18.

20. Sullivan, Peggy. "Children's Library Services." In *ALA Yearbook: A Review of Library Events, 1976.* Chicago: American Library Association, 1977.

21. Baker, Augusta, and Greene, Ellin. *Storytelling: Art and Technique.* New York: R. R. Bowker Co., 1977.

22. Bauer, Caroline Feller. *Handbook for Storytellers.* Chicago: American Library Association, 1977.

23. Pellowski, Anne. *The World of Storytelling.* New York: R. R. Bowker Co., 1977.

24. Harmetz, Richard. "ACFC's Goal: Excellent Films for Youth." *Children's Film International,* no. 1. Los Angeles: University of Southern California, School of Library Science, 1977.

25. Amato, Anthony; Emans, Robert; and Ziegler, Elsie. "Effectiveness of Creative Dramatics and Storytelling in a Library Setting." *Journal of Educational Research* 67 (December 1973): 161–62, 181.

26. Zweizig, Douglas, and Dervin, Brenda. "Public Library Use, Users, Uses: Advances in Knowledge of the Characteristics and Needs of the Adult Clientele of American Public Libraries." In *Advances in Librarianship,* edited by Melvin J. Voigt and Michael H. Harris. Vol. 7. New York: Academic Press, 1977.

27. Barass, Reitzel & Associates, Inc. *A Study of Exemplary Public Library Reading and Reading Related Programs for Children, Youth and Adults.* Vol. 1. Cambridge, Mass.: Barass, Reitzel & Associates, Inc., 1972.

28. Lord, Julia Wood. "Cosmic World of Childhood: The Ideology of the Children's Librarians, 1900–1965. Ph.D. dissertation, Emory University, 1968.

RECENT DEVELOPMENTS IN THE PROVISION OF PUBLIC LIBRARY SERVICES IN THE UNITED KINGDOM

Lorna Paulin

Background

To set the scene, I should like to begin with a few general comments. The older I get, the more clearly I realize that the provision of any public service (and no doubt the provision of most other things in our society too) has to fit in with the ethos of the times. There are such things as general trends in our way of living, although they can seldom be precisely defined and it is often very difficult to say how or why they get started. Thus, much of what is happening in British public libraries today naturally reflects the general trends and the attitudes of mind in most other walks of life. To give just one example of this to begin with, libraries are working much less in isolation than they used to. They are called upon more and more to work closely with all organizations providing cultural services—with education, with health and social services, and with the various services, public and voluntary, that provide information for people. Contact between libraries and the book trade is now much closer, and certainly the concept of all types of library— public, academic, and special—being aspects of one single total service is far more generally accepted than it used to be. This is not a new trend, but there is no doubt that recently it has gathered momentum. One reason for this is economic. When money is scarce, there must be a closing of the ranks and the greatest possible use must be made of all the resources available. But I do not think that this is by any means the only reason. There is, in addition, a welcome tendency to think of the needs of individuals and communities and the provision of all services as a whole instead of in separate watertight compartments.

Considering that almost total responsibility for public library services is in the hands of the local authorities, with hardly any central guidance (and what there is cannot in practice be enforced), it is interesting to observe that public libraries in Britain are tending to develop along roughly similar lines throughout the country. True, we have a Minister for the Arts who is responsible to the Secretary of State for Education

129

and Science and who is officially concerned with public libraries in England and Wales. And there are two Library Advisory Councils, one for England and one for Wales, who no doubt are working hard and who sometimes produce useful reports, but no one can say that public relations are their strong point. Their main function, according to the Public Libraries and Museums Act of 1964 under which they were set up, is to advise the Secretary of State concerning "the provision or use of library facilities." However, when any local authorities are found to be neglecting their library services and the Secretary of State is advised accordingly he is unable at present to insist that such authorities increase their public expenditure. Matters currently under consideration by the Library Advisory Council for England are new media in libraries, library services for a multi-cultural society, library services to the disadvantaged, local library cooperation, and public library management research. Incidentally I find it interesting to see that, although this Council was set up under a Public Libraries Act, only four of its nineteen present members are public librarians; the others are academic and special librarians, members of local authorities, a county education officer, etc. In the British context it is impossible to consider just one type of library without bringing all the others in.

From what I have said you will understand that any national planning for library services in Britain is more likely to come from the consensus of the librarians themselves, including those at the recently established British Library, than from government decisions. No Act of Parliament specifically concerned with public libraries has been passed since 1964, and the provisions of that Act have to some extent been overtaken by events. However certain other Acts, and some Departmental statements, do affect libraries indirectly. One obvious example is the Chronic Sick and Disabled Persons Act of 1970, which specifically includes library services among those which should be provided for the chronic sick and disabled. This has stimulated the development of appropriate services by library authorities in cooperation with their social service departments and the health authorities, but the clauses of the Act are not yet all fully implemented throughout the land. The passing of the Act, however, is in itself indicative of an increasing concern with handicapped people. It is now a statutory requirement that all new public buildings be easily accessible for people in wheelchairs, and a great many older buildings also have been similarly adapted. The provision of library services to the homes of housebound readers is now so general as to be almost universal (it is sometimes done, especially in the rural areas, with the help of volunteers), and I have not seen a public library for years that did not have a good selection of books in large print on its shelves for readers with impaired sight.

Local Government Reorganization

But it is time I gave you some factual statements, so that you can have something definite to go on in considering the general comments I have made. The whole of local government in England and Wales, outside London, and with it of course the public library service, was reorganized completely by an Act of Parliament passed in 1972—the Local Government Act—which came into force on April 1, 1974. Reorganization in Northern Ireland had occurred in 1972. In Scotland it came in 1975; in London it had taken place nearly ten years earlier, in 1965. In England and Wales (population about 50 million) there are now the Greater London Council plus six other metropolitan counties, which are the largest conurbations in those countries, and forty-seven nonmetropolitan counties (often called "shire counties") covering the rest of the country. The average population of the shire counties is about 600,000. Within the Greater London Council area there are the City of London and thirty-two London boroughs. The other six metropolitan counties contain altogether thirty-six districts (average population about 250,000–300,000). The shire counties are also divided into districts, but these have considerably fewer powers than those in the metropolitan counties. All shire counties, all metropolitan districts, and all London boroughs are library authorities, and except in inner London they are also responsible for education.

In England no district within a shire county is a library authority. According to the Local Government Act the same was to apply to Wales, but after much argument the four largest districts in that country have been allowed independent library powers. The government now proposes to transfer the responsibilities for higher and further education in Wales, including public libraries, from the Department of Education and Science to the Welsh Office. This is in accordance with a general trend toward some devolution of powers within the United Kingdom, but at present it seems unlikely that the provision of public libraries will be significantly changed by it. The net result of local government reorganization in England and Wales is that the number of separate library authorities has been reduced from 385 to 121, and there are no small library authorities—a situation that many of us worked for for many years.

The importance of making the same authorities responsible for education and library services was stressed over and over again in the parliamentary debates before the Local Government Act was passed. However, contrary to most professional advice, this principle was not adhered to in the corresponding Act relating to Scotland (population about 5.5 million), the Local Government (Scotland) Act, 1973. Here, local government reorganization has resulted in a system of regional councils (which are education authorities) with their areas divided into districts, and library powers have gone to the districts except in those parts of the country that are very sparsely populated. The total number of library authorities in Scotland nevertheless has been halved, from eighty to forty (three regions, three groups of islands, and thirty-four districts). Moreover, whereas each of thirty-seven authorities formerly served less than 20,000 population, there are now only six with a population of under 50,000. In Scotland libraries on the whole are grouped with leisure, recreation, and amenity services for administrative purposes.

In Northern Ireland the system is different again (but of course). Five autonomous Education and Library Area Boards have been set up, reporting directly to the government of the province. They serve, respectively, the city of Belfast and the North East, South East, South, and West of the country. This form of organization meets with general professional satisfaction, but it is unpopular among politicians. Two of the four major parties are threatening to disband it or at least to alter it substantially, and certainly any political settlement that might be reached in Northern Ireland would almost certainly involve the end of these officially appointed (not elected) boards. There are at present, then, five library authorities in Northern Ireland instead of the former sixteen, serving the total population of rather more than 1.5 million. Library and educational responsibilities are closely associated for administrative purposes in the Education and Library Area Boards.

In England and Wales the question of whether the public library service is best administered on its own, with education, or with leisure and amenity services has by no means been finally settled. The present pattern is a patchwork. The Library Association has found that the committees governing libraries have no fewer than thirty-five titles between them, such headings as "Amenities," "Education," "Leisure," and even "Libraries" being generally adopted for various groupings of services [1, pp. 18–19]. Similarly, the title of the chief librarian varies a great deal. Fortunately, some are still called City Librarian and County Librarian but some have to put up with, for example, Assistant Director of Leisure Services (Libraries). Along with these changes have gone one or two attempts to downgrade the salary of the chief librarian's post, but such attempts have been firmly withstood by the profession. The duties and the levels of responsibility of the post have rarely been affected by these changes of title, except that the range of duties has sometimes been widened.

At the same time as the reorganization of local government took place in England and Wales, the National Health Service was also thoroughly shaken up. Under the Department of Health and Social Security a system was set up of regions, which are divided into areas, which are divided into districts. The areas are the same as the shire counties, and it was a great relief to find that at last the health service organization was coterminous with other services' areas, at least on one level. This had never happened before, and the difficulty of getting a County Council to work with a Regional Hospital Board that served only a part of its area had hindered the development of hospital library services provided jointly by the two kinds of authority. All seemed set, therefore, for a big step forward in hospital libraries in 1974, but although some progress has been made since then there has been disappointingly little of it owing to lack of money.

Despite its coincidence with a period of financial crisis, local government reorganization has benefited most of the libraries in the country. We no longer have the absurd separation of towns from their surrounding rural areas. In England, Northern Ireland, and most of Wales, the fact that libraries and education are provided by the same authorities is of great advantage to both. Above all, there are no longer any library authorities that are too small to provide an adequate service. It is true that, in a few places where the county library services were much less well developed than those of the larger towns that were forced to join with them, the service to those larger towns became less efficient for a time, but there is no need for this to be more than a temporary phase. The councils of some cities, especially those that used to be education authorities, feel the loss of their powers keenly, and there have been suggestions that certain responsibilities, for education and libraries, for example, should be restored to them. It is to be hoped that these suggestions are not taken seriously. The last thing that our local government needs at present is yet more reorganization. With each year that goes by the new authorities feel more established and more secure in their own identities. Whatever its failings, it is essential that the present organization be given time really to settle down and to work. Some advantages have already become abundantly clear; for example, in the pooling of the resources of the libraries. This not only helps local readers but greatly facilitates the national interlibrary lending system. Many more advantages will follow from reorganization.

Financial Crisis

Since 1974 it has been difficult to say precisely which of the problems confronting local government have resulted from the upheaval of reorganization and which from recurring financial crises. Certainly lack of money has meant that reorganization has hardly had a chance to prove that it was worthwhile. The decision to have a two-tier local government system of counties and districts and to divide powers between them inevitably meant greater total expenditure on administrative staff and on office buildings that did not immediately improve the services to the people, and criticism on that score has been vociferous. However, public libraries have been an exception to this general rule, as they are now more economically provided than under the old regime.

This brings me to the effects of financial crises on the library service. Our present situation is that public libraries are being used more and more. Loans this year have gone up by about 3–5 percent, after an average increase of between 6 and 7 percent last year. Normally no additional staff are being appointed, while actual reductions in staff have been made by some library authorities. By no means do all authorities allow sufficient additional funds annually to meet increased book prices, which have gone up on average 88 percent in five years. Very few new buildings, or extensions to existing buildings, are being erected. In the shire counties the financial situation is being made worse by the government's policy of diverting funds to the inner-city areas. Socially this may well be the right thing to do, but naturally the counties find it hard to bear. The system is for the government to provide a rate-support grant to all nonmetropolitan county authorities, metropolitan districts, and London boroughs, amounting on average to 61 percent of their total expenditure. This average conceals a very wide variation. Owing to the pressing needs of the inner cities, the rate-support grant for the metropolitan districts is far above the average and rises to as much as 80 percent or even more in city areas with the greatest need. The nonmetropolitan counties, on the other hand, tend to receive far less than the average, and the amount goes down to as low as 40 percent in some counties. The result is, of course, that if the nonmetropolitan counties do no more than maintain their services at the former level, or even if they reduce their standards quite considerably, there is a very noticeable rise in the amounts of the rates (that is, the local taxes) that they have to raise because a reduction in the rate-support grant for a county can easily result in the loss of as much as £5 million–£10 million in one year. No ratepayer likes having to pay more anyway, but when higher rates are combined with lower standards of service the amount of ire in the breast rises accordingly. So some antagonism to local authorities and the way they spend public money has inevitably arisen.

Given this hardly encouraging state of affairs, what is being done? First, naturally enough, there is great emphasis on exploiting to the maximum those resources that we have—and not only those in public libraries. As I mentioned earlier, there is much greater willingness to look at the total provision of library services for a community, whether those services are provided by the public library authority; the education authority for schools, colleges of further education, or polytechnics;

universities; hospitals; or large industrial and commercial firms. Regular meetings between *all* the librarians of *all* types of library within a town are found to be extremely useful, especially in relation to the sharing of resources, cooperation in the purchase of expensive material, and in the storage of reserve stocks.

Luckily, many public library authorities made hay while the sun shone in the 1960s and the early 1970s, when book funds increased rapidly, more staff were appointed, and many good new buildings were achieved. With the changes brought about by local government reorganization these buildings are perhaps not all in the places one would have chosen, but the fullest advantage is being taken of them nonetheless. On the whole, therefore, public libraries are maintaining services at a fairly acceptable level, but there has been retrenchment and the whole situation is sadly different from that of a decade ago, when expansion, development and improvement were the order of the day. What does not diminish is the desire of readers for a good service and the frustration of librarians who see clearly what developments are needed and how beneficial they would be but who are unable to act accordingly.

By no means do all of our local authorities realize the value of public library services. In times of financial crisis there is a real danger such authorities will cut libraries' funds disproportionately, while the services that are of more obvious importance, such as the provision of roads, certain social services for the disadvantaged, and formal education, are treated more gently. It is hard for librarians to tolerate this, if only because library funds represent a tiny proportion of the expenditure of a local authority and no cuts in them, however severe and damaging to the service, can make an appreciable difference to the amount of rates levied. In counties surrounding London, for example, on average only about 1.56 percent of total local government expenditure is devoted to libraries. If library services were to be closed down altogether, no one would even notice the effect on the rates he has to pay, but the sad effect on the quality of life would be very noticeable indeed. Moreover, as we know so well, the library service is one of the cheapest ways we have of providing education, information, and recreation, for we give readers the resources to use on a "do-it-yourself" basis. It would be sensible, therefore, to develop libraries and actually to increase the services they provide and cut down expenditure on other services which cost incomparably more; I must admit that I see little chance of this being done.

Responses to Library Cuts

The Library Association is keenly aware of the danger that libraries will be made to take more than their fair share of cuts. In October 1975 the

Council issued a statement on library and information services in a time of economic crisis. In this statement the Library Association said that it did not expect libraries to be exempt from all cuts in expenditure, but it emphasized the increased importance of public libraries in times of economic difficulty and the need to avoid causing serious damage to the service by any disproportionately great reductions. The statement which was widely circulated to those most likely to be concerned was expressed in the courteous and somewhat cautious language that is perhaps to be expected from a professional association operating under a Royal Charter. You will not be surprised to hear that some librarians, mostly young ones, have formed a group which expresses itself less temperately. This group is called "Libraries against the cuts," and it holds meetings and produces the widely circulated *Libraries against the Cuts Bulletin* giving detailed information on cuts that are being made and about the petitions and demonstrations against them. It is prepared to initiate trade-union activity against cuts and give advice on running a local campaign of protest.

Every effort is being made to see that the government is aware of the dangers, actual or potential, of the present situation. It is apparent that the messages are getting through, as was clear when (some months after receiving a deputation from the Library Association) Lord Donaldson, minister for the arts, addressed the Association's annual conference in September 1976. He spoke at some length on the subject of budget cuts and said that it would be shortsighted and mistaken for greater cuts to be imposed on library services than were their fair share. "You must fight back if you are suffering disproportionately," he said. "What you and I have got to do is try to make sure that we can go most of the way to maintain standards even if we can't increase them." Later he added, "We are going to win this war, no matter how many battles may go against us on the way." He affirmed, however, that he had no intention of interfering with local decisions on priorities [2, p. 468].

There is much to be said for having a considerable measure of local autonomy, but if local authorities behave irresponsibly there can be a heavy price to be paid by the people who are not provided with the services they need. A rather stronger line than that taken by the Minister for the Arts has recently been expressed by his superior at the Ministry, the Secretary of State for Education and Science, Shirley Williams. The rate-support grant is made up of allocations of funds intended by the government for the various individual services. It has been found that a few authorities are diverting to other purposes that portion of the grant intended for libraries, and that during 1976–77 there was actually an underspending of £2 million of the libraries' share. Williams was perturbed to see this, and she has warned the authorities that if funds intended for one service are not used for that service they may be withheld by the government altogether. Moreover any underspending adversely affects the amount available for the ensuing year.

The Secretary of the Library Association, Robert Hilliard, in a published statement has referred to the wider implications of any undue reduction in funds for libraries [3]. He points out that even apart from the great importance of libraries in primary, secondary, and tertiary education and for the public as a whole they have a vital part to play in the economic prosperity of the country by providing information services. Moreover, any serious reductions in book funds can adversely affect the publishing industry, which is a substantial export industry making a valuable contribution to the national balance of payments. In logic and plain common sense all Hilliard's arguments are unanswerable. But which country is governed, nationally or locally, strictly in accordance with logic and plain common sense?

The current financial situation regarding libraries throughout the country and the struggles (and often the great ingenuity) of librarians and their committees to minimize the effects of cuts in expenditure are being fairly well documented. The Library Association surveys the position from time to time, and during 1977 the Branch and Mobile Libraries Group published in their journal, *Service Point*, a series of statements by chief librarians explaining briefly the nature of the economies that they were being required to make and the philosophy underlying their actions [4, 5]. It is an interesting experience to read these statements. In one or two respects diametrically opposed philosophies are expounded. The majority of librarians, for example, try to defend their book funds at almost all costs, owing to the cumulative effect of any serious erosion there, but some take the opposite view. The librarian of Oldham in the metropolitan county of Greater Manchester says: "An inadequate bookfund is the surest way to kill a good service but the need for quick savings often makes prophecies of doom sound impertinent" [4, p. 25]. In Buckinghamshire and Surrey, on the other hand, two authorities that have cut back their library services particularly severely, the book funds have suffered more than any other aspects of expenditure.

The statement by the librarian of Cheshire, where the value of the library service is properly appreciated by the council, is typical of the line being taken by the majority of authorities:

New Cheshire started life in April 1974 with great problems and even greater ambitions. The problems were to integrate eleven library systems and to replace seven major libraries as well as building a number of branch libraries and doubling the transport fleet. The ambitions were to create a corporate library and information service which would include local government information, community information, service to the Area Health Authority, service to industry and integration of the work of all information and advice agencies in the County. Progress has been made in certain directions and the expenditure of the Authority expanded considerably in 1974/5 and to some extent in 1975/6. However, the underlying trend for economy has caused reductions in staffing which resulted in cuts in opening hours of branch and district libraries (including Saturday afternoons), whilst the bookfund has been unprotected in 1976/7 from the effects of inflation which are estimated at £113,000. Cheshire Libraries are preparing in 1977/8 to be virtually frozen as to a cash basis from the previous year, but with commitments for growth from the residual capital programme. In an effort to improve income, fines and reservations charges have been doubled, charges introduced for borrowing sound recordings, and book sales are being held regularly. Instead of bemoaning our fate, we are trying to find more effective ways of spending the reduced bookfund by way of better book provision, stock control and user surveys. [5, p. 21]

Economizing by reducing the libraries' hours of opening is unfortunately becoming a fairly general practice. If hours have to be reduced, obviously most readers would be put to comparatively little inconvenience if libraries closed for part or the whole of Monday. That, however, would not save as much money as Saturday closing, because in recent years the unions have been successful at the national level in obtaining extra pay for local government employees who work what are described as "unsocial hours"—which include late evenings and Saturdays. It was presumably thought when negotiations for extra pay were concluded that public libraries would always be kept open on Saturdays, when they are in greatest demand, but it is never safe to forecast what local authorities will do. So far, libraries still almost universally open on Saturday mornings, but too many of them now close at midday. It is a classic case of being hoist with one's own petard. The unions negotiated extra pay for the staff for Saturday working, therefore if the authorities had to save money they shut libraries on Saturday afternoons. The net result is that the staff do not get the extra pay and the readers do not get the service they need either. It is very easy to think that once the hours of opening have been restricted in this way they will never be increased again, but I am thankful to say that there are already signs that there may be some improvement before very long. Cheshire, in fact, hopes to restore Saturday afternoon opening in 1979.

Some authorities are trying to economize by closing branch libraries that are not used very much. This, however, often arouses public opposition, and the long-suffering people have been known to rise up and protest. An example of this occurred in the London Borough of Kensington and Chelsea, where the librarian reports:

There was a gratifying response from the public—particularly children at local schools—when news of the one library closure (the Kensal part-time branch) was released. Children sent petitions and letters in their own hand to the Leader of the Council, telling him that their library visit was their most enjoyable experience of the week in that socially deprived part of the Borough in which they live. The Leader of the Council took particular personal interest in this matter and became convinced that the maintenance of a service at the branch for the particular use of children and the elderly should be considered. When the Libraries and Amenities Committee were told that the library could be retained, and that the full savings would not therefore be required, this welcome evidence of community reaction to an appreciated and often under-estimated public service was well received. [4, p. 22–23]

A better way of saving money than by closing libraries can be by a measure of rationalization whereby the function of each individual library within a system is gauged as precisely as possible and every library does not try to do everything. It is becoming more usual, for example, for the main stock of fairly specialized material such as music, advanced technological literature, and books in foreign languages to be concentrated in those libraries within a system where it is most used. It is available throughout the system on request, and its existence is often indicated by circulating displays or very small representative selections to all service points. In my own county of Hertfordshire, we deliberately made a few branches "popular libraries," with the more advanced material removed from their permanent stock but readily supplied, when needed, from the nearest large library within the system.

Buildings

Capital development is at present almost at a standstill. Few if any new library buildings are being permitted to start, although some that were being built at the time of the financial crisis are gradually being completed and opened. They are all greatly needed, but when no additional funds can be allocated to maintaining them they can become a serious drain on a library's resources. Readers invariably make full and enthusiastic use of them, which means that resources of staff and books may have to be diverted from older established libraries within the system, where they can be spared only with great difficulty. New buildings, in other words, however desirable and indeed necessary, can at present be a mixed blessing. Spurred on at least partly by the lack of money, there are, naturally enough, some libraries being housed in newly converted buildings. These can prove to be very satisfactory—for example, in Nottingham where a former furniture shop right in the middle of the city is now the central library. The site could not be bettered, and it would never have been available for a purpose-built library.

It appears that funds for new buildings will be inadequate for several years to come. Local authorities finance capital development of this kind by raising loans, normally through the Public Works Loan Board, and the government controls the total sum that may be raised. The Department of Education and Science has recently supplied the Library

Association with a detailed breakdown of a public expenditure forecast for libraries for each year to 1980–81 [6, table 2.10]. This indicates a steady if small growth in current expenditure on public libraries but a severe cutback in provisions for capital expenditure (from £11.6 million in 1976–77—a sum which was far less than was required—to no more than £2.2 million in 1980–81).

Where libraries are inadequately housed, and a good many are in spite of the achievements of the past fifteen years, they will simply have to concentrate on more extramural work in the community itself and in cooperation with schools and colleges. In some areas mobile libraries, usually of trailer type, are temporarily providing a service until buildings can be obtained. These can be reasonably satisfactory, especially in smaller communities, but they necessarily concentrate on lending services only. Container libraries, which were pioneered a few years ago in Cornwall, are also being used in some appropriate areas. They have considerably more floor space than any mobile libraries, being in fact like mobile buildings, and the normal arrangement is for them to be transported overnight and then left on one site for perhaps a couple of days, being connected with all utility services while they are there. Container libraries are very much cheaper than permanent buildings, and they are as economical in staff and book stock as mobile libraries as both are constantly in action.

Book Sales

You will have observed from the statement by the librarian of Cheshire that attempts are being made to increase the library's income by raising fines and book reservation charges and holding sales of books that are no longer required. The great majority of library authorities are doing the same sort of thing. It used to be thought that public libraries could not sell their books as this would not be in accordance with the Library Licence Agreement, arrived at by the Library Association, the Publishers Association, and the Booksellers Association, under which all public libraries obtain their books at 10 percent discount. C. R. Eastwood, the county librarian of Somerset, doubted the validity of this belief, and it is thanks to his patient and dogged pursuit of the matter that it has now been established that public library book stock may be sold. The book sales that are being held are remarkably popular with the public, and I have not heard of any objections from booksellers. Some authorities put withdrawn books constantly on sale, others hold sales for perhaps one week each month. Children's books and adult nonfiction are in greatest demand. All books are sold at very much below the published price— usually 10 percent for fiction and children's books and rather more, perhaps up to 20 percent for adult nonfiction. The amount of the income from these book sales and from selling book lists, pamphlets, reproductions of old prints of local buildings, badges for children, etc., is not great. Indeed, even including increased fines and reservation charges and charges for the hiring of library rooms the total amount of a library's income is very unlikely to be more than about 5 percent of its expenditure, so that its effect on local authorities is psychological rather than actual. The value of the psychological effect on a finance committee should not, however, be underrated.

Paperback Books

Even where book funds have more or less kept pace with rising prices, or at least have not been severely cut, it is increasingly the custom in British libraries to buy large numbers of books in paperback form. This is by no means a new idea. My own authority, Hertfordshire, was doing it on a considerable scale over ten years ago, not because of lack of money at that time but because we thought the books would be attractive to teenagers whom we wanted to encourage to come to the library. We were successful in that aim but we found that a great many readers, not only teenagers, liked paperbacks better than hardbacks. From that time as a matter of policy the stock of all libraries in the county contained a large proportion of paperbacks. To begin with the books were reinforced, but we soon realized that this was seldom necessary. Even ten years ago it was of course helpful to make the book fund go as far as possible, and I was surprised then as I have been since at the strength of the resistance among some librarians to the purchase of paperbacks. This resistance has now been forced to crumble, and it is one result of the restriction on funds that many readers will welcome.

Staffing

The largest single item on any library's budget is normally staff salaries, and it is in the employment of staff that many of our libraries face their biggest problems at present. Several libraries are not allowed to fill any vacancies that occur, and this results in unsatisfactorily haphazard staffing arrangements. Some are required to reduce their establishments, normally by "natural wastage" rather than by declaring staff redundant. Much thought is having to be given to streamlining the libraries' methods and to cutting out all unnecessarily laborious processes. A particularly regrettable tendency is to cut out all trainee schemes. Under these schemes members of staff are appointed in addition to the normal establishment and, after receiving some training in the library, are sent on full salary to schools of librarianship to study full-time before returning to posts in their employing libraries. These schemes have proved to be highly beneficial to the students and libraries concerned, but there is no denying that they are expensive. Very few operate at present, but the general policy in individual libraries is to leave such a scheme on ice rather than to remove it from the establishment altogether, so that it can be "unfrozen" and put into effect again as soon as times improve. The ill effects of the absence of trainee schemes for at least the next few years will unfortunately be felt in the long term and not immediately, and local authorities find it temptingly easy to be shortsighted in these matters.

I do not wish to give the impression that all is at present doom and gloom in British public libraries. One hears a lot about those authorities who are cutting their services back severely, but very little about the numerous places where libraries are being maintained reasonably well. Perhaps the latter fear to draw attention to themselves, thereby tempting providence (and their councils). Even though the present rate of progress cannot be what we should wish, the service given nearly everywhere is undoubtedly better than it was, say, ten years ago. Maintaining services at the level they have recently attained presents a challenge, and it is encouraging to see that many librarians are taking up the challenge not only bravely but enthusiastically, and sometimes even successfully. To give but two examples. The librarian of the Royal Borough of Croydon writes: "Speaking personally, I wonder why I am not fed up when I seem to spend most of my time not planning new developments but fighting to keep my defeats to a minimum, but I am not—sweet are the uses of adversity (well, some of them)" [5, p. 27]. And the librarian of Leicestershire is also thinking of the uses of adversity when he writes: "No one likes making economies but they make us think, and count, and for Leicestershire they are yet another stimulus to produce a library service in town and country tailored to meet community needs and providing the user with access to county-wide and national resources of books, other media and information" [5, p. 31].

Technological Innovation

Fortuitously, the introduction of some technological innovation has been spurred on by the need to economize on staff time (just as, long ago, labor-saving equipment in the home was devised when domestic help was no longer obtainable). Rapid development in this sphere was taking place in any case, and two periodicals in particular are helpful in providing up-to-date information on what is currently going on in the

United Kingdom. They are *Program: News of Computers in Libraries,* published quarterly by Aslib, 3 Belgrave' Square, London, and *VINE: Very Informal Newsletter on Library Automation,* which appears irregularly and is edited by Philip J. D. Bramall, information officer for library automation, who is based at the Library of the University of Southampton.

In the context of public libraries, rather than that of the library service of the country as a whole, the application of computers to library housekeeping has made great progress during the last decade. As always, a few libraries pioneered such developments, and others who started later were able to profit from the pioneers' successes and failures and also to save themselves considerable expense. It was certainly prudent not to rush in too early, as computer science itself was making giant strides and equipment was liable to become out of date very quickly. As a computer expert remarked at the time, "If it works, it's obsolete." However, things have now reached the stage where at least some measure of computerization in a large public library system (and we have no small ones) is a natural step to take. In 1976 it was found that 170 libraries and information units had operational computerized systems, and fifty-one of these were public libraries [7]; the number has increased almost month by month ever since. The majority of libraries use computers and computer staff belonging to the parent organizations. This can often be done at no extra cost to the libraries' own budgets, but of course it is at a cost to the parent body. A few libraries, such as the Birmingham Libraries Co-operative Mechanisation Project, have bought computer time at commerical rates from computer bureaus [8, pp. 321–22]. An increasing number of libraries are buying their own minicomputers, a recent example being Derbyshire [9, 10], which has just gone on-line with a fully automated library system involving acquisitions, cataloging, circulation control, stock control, reservation control, and borrowers' register. Derbyshire claims that such a full system, which is on-line at all times during library hours, has not been available before in the United Kingdom or indeed, with the same specifications, in the rest of the world.

The computerization of just one or two processes within a library reduces the workload for overburdened staff. It can be self-financing, and it can even mean a saving of money, if fewer staff are needed. It is in order to reduce administrative costs that Oldham, for example, has decided to extend its computer-based circulation system to branch libraries still using a manual method. Westminster was able to release two clerical posts by computerizing its catalog, and in spite of being forced to make economies Leicestershire is carrying through a library automation program which by 1979 will have its six major libraries within a computerized network and all their stocks on a microfilm catalog. It is interesting to note that in the county of Clwyd, in Wales, help in computerization has been obtained in the processing for catalog integration following on local government reorganization from the government's Manpower Services Commission's Job Creation Scheme. Eighteen assistants were acquired under this scheme, which is intended to give employment for a limited period to people who would otherwise be unemployed.

I have emphasized the development of domestic computerization, as it were, for housekeeping jobs within individual library systems. It will be clear to you that public libraries, like libraries of all other types, are much affected and helped by computerized information services on a national and international scale. BLAISE (the British Library Automated Information Service), for example, has been operational since the middle of 1977, and at the moment provides access to such data bases as MARC; Medline, Toxline, and other data bases provided by the U.S. National Library of Medicine; and those of some other U.S. institutions such as the National Institute for Occupational Safety and Health (NIOSH) [11, pp. 26–27].

Library and Information Science Abstracts (LISA) went on-line in June 1977 with the System Development Corporation System (SDC), service to the public being made available by SDC and Lockheed. Which reminds me that at one of my own libraries, at Stevenage in Hertfordshire, as long ago as 1975 we installed a computer terminal for interrogating data bases available through Lockheed Dialog and other data bases, and so far as I know this was the first public library in Britain to do so. We found that it saved us money, as we no longer had to take and file various published indexing and abstracting services.

Public libraries will also no doubt be frequent users of the Viewdata system that is being introduced by the British Post Office [12–15]. This is an information storage and retrieval system, using the ordinary telephone system which is linked to the television receiver to transmit information held in a central computer. It is designed to serve the general public as well as the business community, and it will be very simple to operate, using a numeric hand-held keypad to select information, guided by instructions displayed on the screen. The range of subjects to be covered is extremely wide, from the Stock Exchange and company and market information to cars, sport, holidays, and the weather. The Post Office has been running a pilot trial since January 1976, and a market trial is to begin in June 1978 in London, Birmingham, and Norwich, when some 1,000 users will be invited to take part in a small-scale service. A limited public service may, it is hoped, be implemented before the end of 1979. The implications of Viewdata are being earnestly discussed by librarians at meetings and courses.

A less welcome form of technological innovation that is being introduced into some of our public libraries is aimed at preventing the unauthorized removal of books, whether inadvertently or deliberately. Various systems, such as Checkpoint and Tattletape, have been imported from the United States for this purpose. The problem of book theft has arisen, oddly enough, in only a few public libraries so far, and it is difficult to say why it should occur in some places and not others. On the whole, university and college libraries suffer more than public libraries in this respect, which would appear to be a sad comment on what higher education does for people.

Networking

A further topic that was included in my brief, but which I have hardly referred to so far, is networking. As you know, this has for a very long time been fairly highly developed in the United Kingdom, which is, comparatively speaking, a very compact, densely populated area where interlibrary cooperation is obviously desirable and relatively easy to put into practice. Since local government reorganization and the great reduction in the number of separate public library authorities it has become yet easier. Nevertheless complications arise, and it is natural to ask whether the old, established system of national interlending plus interlending within regional areas of the country, each with a regional bureau to organize the work, should be continued, especially now that the British Library Lending Division in Yorkshire has developed the direct lending of books, serials, and photocopies to local libraries. A working party set up by the National Committee on Regional Library Co-operation to consider the future pattern of interlending produced a report in December 1977 [16]. In it the opinion was expressed that it would be wise to develop and exploit the respective strengths of the British Library Lending Division and the regional cooperation systems in order to prevent wasteful duplication, and the report defined respective strengths. Further studies to ascertain the potential demands that would be made upon regional schemes were proposed. These studies are particularly necessary, as a far-reaching effect on library cooperation is expected both from the development of BLAISE, Viewdata, and other automated systems for the direct supply of information and from the growth of direct lending from the British Library Lending Division, which by-pass former interlending arrangements. Meanwhile some former subject specialization schemes among regional groupings of libraries, such as the scheme in London and the South East which is the most comprehensive, have been revised, and it is clear that they are still of value [17, pp. 13–15]. Incidentally, an enormous amount of interlibrary lending, both nationally and within the regional groupings, takes place. In the London and South Eastern region alone about 250,000 requests for interlending are dealt with every year.

To turn to quite a different aspect of cooperation, interlibrary road transport on a cooperative basis has been considered. A pilot scheme was tried in the northwest of England, initially financed by the British Library Research and Development Department, and then another based in London was set up for nine months, in March 1977 [18, 19]. This is working so well that it has been decided to continue it for at least a further year. The London scheme operates at the rate of over half a million items carried per annum using eleven vans, and over 97 percent of all items are delivered on the same day or the day after collection. The items are being lent between the libraries in the London area and from the British Library Lending Division in Yorkshire. The scheme is being run on a cost-recovery basis with the participating libraries sharing the cost, which amounts to about £110,000 a year. The British Library Research and Development Department is considering the feasibility of a national scheme, using road and rail transport jointly, but the results of the two pilot schemes are to be studied carefully first.

Schemes of local cooperation or networking between libraries of different types within one city, conurbation, or county, particularly in relation to technological literature, have been part of the British Library scene for at least three decades. They continue to flourish, and in September 1977 yet another was added to the list. It is called "Network" [20] and has been set up in order to coordinate and develop the library service in the fields of commerce, science, and technology in Northumberland, Durham, and Tyne and Wear areas. The system uses all public libraries involved as access points, and there is what is described as "agreed interest and co-operation" from Durham University, Newcastle Polytechnic, Newcastle University, and Sunderland Polytechnic. This new scheme is similar in many ways to various other local schemes that are working successfully, each one being tailored to fit the specific needs of its own locality.

Conclusion

It is time to draw together this attempt to describe the current state of public libraries in the United Kingdom. Wherever you look, you see national concerns reflected, whether clearly or faintly, in what public libraries are doing. Thus there is concern for, and help with, the government's adult literacy campaign; specific provision, as a matter of agreed policy, for ethnic minorities; regard to the needs of unemployed people in using the time they unwillingly have on their hands; and greatly increasing emphasis on information services. In fact the last-mentioned topic is of considerable concern both nationally and locally, as the number of agencies providing information of importance to citizens in their everyday life has proliferated to a bewildering extent and there is an urgent need for them to be coordinated and, where necessary, supplemented. There could be no better organization to do this than the public library which is centrally and conveniently situated, open when people are free to visit it, and with an objective that has been recently defined and generally accepted, as "to bring to the individual/group accurate information quickly and in depth, particularly on topics of current concern" [21]. Of all the many and varied activities of public libraries that have pressing claims for priority, this function is a good candidate for being priority number one in our country at present.

The total coverage of the United Kingdom with public library services is, and has been for many years, such that very few if any of the population are out of reach of a reasonably convenient service point. That battle, so far as it goes, was won long ago. What we have to do now is fight to maintain the standard of what each reader finds in his service point when he gets there. And before very long, we devoutly hope, we shall not only maintain the standard but raise it to a very much higher level than it now reaches.

REFERENCES

1. Whatley, H. A., ed. *British Librarianship and Information Science 1971–1975*. London: Library Association, 1977.
2. "Fight Back against Unfair Cuts, Advises Minister." *Library Association Record* 78 (October 1976): 468.
3. *Bookseller* (February 28, 1976), p. 1415.
4. "Surviving the Cuts." *Service Point* (September 1977) pp. 16–35.
5. "Surviving the Cuts." *Service Point* (April 1977), pp. 21–35.
6. Great Britain. Treasury. *The Government's Expenditure Plans Presented to Parliament by the Chancellor of the Exchequer*. Cmnd. 6721, I and II. London: HMSO, 1977.
7. Wilson, C. W. J., ed. *Directory of Operational Computer Applications in United Kingdom Libraries and Information Units*. 2d ed. London: Aslib, 1976.
8. Lynch, Michael F., and Adamson, George W. "The Impact of the Computer." In *British Librarianship Today*, edited by Wilfred L. Saunders. London: Library Association, 1976.
9. Gratton, Peter, and Field, Roy. "Reducing the Need for Human Decisions." *Library Association Record* 79 (July 1977): 372–73.
10. "Derbyshire County Libraries: On-Line Circulation Control to be Added to Existing Interactive Services." *VINE* (January 1977), pp. 40–42.
11. British Library. *Fourth Annual Report 1976–1977*. London: British Library, 1977.
12. Fedida, S. "Screened Information at the Touch of a Button." *Post Office Telecommunications Journal* 27 (Winter 1975): 4–6.
13. Fedida, S. "Viewdata: The Post Office's Textual Information and Communications System." *Wireless World* 83 (February 1977): 32–34, (March 1977): 52–54, (April 1977): 65–69, (May 1977): 55–59.

14. Fedida, S. "Viewdata : A Post Office Interactive Information Medium for the General Public." *Electronics and Power* 23 (June 1977): 467–73.
15. Valery, Michael. "Foot in the Door for the Home Computer." *New Scientist* 74 (April 14, 1977): 63–65.
16. National Committee on Regional Library Co-operation. *Report of the Working Party on the Future Pattern of Interlending.* London: National Committee on Regional Library Co-operation, 1977.
17. London and South Eastern Library Region. *Annual Report 1975–76.* London: London and South Eastern Library Region, 1976.
18. Local Government Operational Research Unit. *A Pilot Transport Scheme for Inter-Library Loans in the North West.* London: Royal Institute of Public Administration, 1977.
19. Local Government Operational Research Unit. *A Pilot Transport Scheme for Inter-Library Loans in London.* London: Royal Institute of Public Administration, 1977.
20. "Network: A New Library Co-operative Scheme." *North East Libraries Bulletin* (November 1977), pp. 3–4.
21. Library Association, London and Home Counties Branch, Public Library Research Group. "Public Library Aims and Objectives." *Library Association Record* 73 (December 1971): 233–34.

PROSPECTS FOR AND EFFECTING CHANGE IN THE PUBLIC LIBRARY

Robert Wedgeworth

A Nineteenth-Century Public Library

Perhaps the most enduring quality of the public library has been its ability to survive the dramatic changes which have affected its communications setting, its governmental relations, the technology of librarianship and, of course, its users. Yet the institution has survived remarkably unchanged in character from its late nineteenth-century prototype. It is quite possible that Dewey or Poole could walk into the average public library today and find its atmosphere quite familiar.

Since most of the public library buildings in this country were built in the first half of this century, their classical architectural style would be well known to them. A casual stroll through the stacks would reveal a largely monographic collection with substantial bound periodical holdings. Access to this literature would still be primarily through the dictionary card catalog and printed indexes to literature. Looking carefully, they might come upon a phonograph record collection or other nonprint materials. However, because usually unobtrusively located, these materials and equipment might not disconcert them. A peek into the technical services areas would more than likely reveal a familiar world of books, typewriters, and various desks and card files. A computer terminal might be puzzling until upon closer examination they saw the system output of 3×5-inch catalog cards. Strolling back into the reading rooms, they would not likely be disturbed or interrupted by any of the librarians or assistants waiting to be consulted behind their desks. In essence, a corner of nineteenth-century familiarity would offer reassurance after a rush of modern sounds and sights that would be nothing short of astounding to our visitors from the past.

Problems Raised by the Conference Papers

During this conference, we have examined the responses made by the public library to the major driving forces for change in its environment. Given the overwhelming complexity of the modern communications setting, the need for the public library to intervene in the process of information dissemination has been questioned. Indeed, the lack of understanding by public librarians of the structure and dynamics of this setting and how it affects the lives of those who live in it have hampered efforts to determine what information people need and why. Certainly, there is little relationship between the laudable educational and cultural objectives of the public library and the most influential communications medium of our time—television. Advertising dominates television, where the sole purpose is to persuade viewers to consume products and services to fulfill needs that are frequently induced by the medium itself.

Public librarians face a general environment in which their claims to their two most enduring objectives, education and recreation, have been considerably eroded. The resources for the first have been curtailed by the dominance of the formal education establishment, while the enormous changes wrought by the media within our society have made the recreational contributions of public libraries less meaningful to the average citizen.

The advent of new technology has presented a broadened range of complexities in the administration of the public library, as well as obscuring the definition of appropriate services for its various users. At the same time, there have been spiraling increases in the total expenses of public libraries, while their incomes have either stabilized or declined. Even when stabilized, the purchasing power of their incomes has declined considerably because, in the ten-year period between 1967 and 1977, the average cost of books and periodicals has gone up 114 percent and 207 percent, respectively. If one adds to this the move toward larger units, the possibilities of economies of scale, and the development of complex nationwide bibliographic networks, a sense of the range of problems which public libraries are attempting to face today becomes possible.

Yet public libraries continue to have strong services for children. The emphasis in children's services on the selection of quality materials and on the recreational objective of library service has drawn considerable attention. This stems partly from the competition of school media centers as well as pressures to reallocate the resources of the public library. Some public library administrators assert that children's services can be handled more effectively through schools because they are in contact with far more children than the public library [1, p. 45]. This position tends to ignore the fact that although the growth of services in school libraries and media centers has been phenomenal, many schools still lack adequate facilities to provide these services.

However, differences over the objectives for children's services constrain a rational development of cooperative activities between school and public libraries. Here too, though, television has had its impact. Such programs as "Sesame Street" and "The Electric Company" have diminished the importance of the recreational objective of public library service to children. However, these programs place little emphasis upon reading maintenance. The obvious relationship between their efforts to assist children to learn how to read has not been related to the need to provide them with the opportunity to continue discovering the delights of reading and at the same time improve their skill.

While public libraries attempt to recapture an adult user group through greater attention to information services—outreach, consumer, health, and welfare—it is the young-adult user group which illustrates most clearly both the weaknesses and the opportunities for service programs for the public library. Young-adult services have emerged on a pragmatic basis with little rationale and even less research upon which to build firm foundations for the service. Although young-adult services are the most recently developed of the major groups of user services, it is no longer acceptable to the field for these services to lack a precise definition based on the dominant characteristics of the target group. Adolescence is a well-researched period of human development with a large corpus of medical and behavioral science literature; yet little of what this literature contains can be found in the library literature.

The fact that young adults as a group have not been very well served by the rigid structure and inflexible programs of the formal educational institutions has not had much impact upon library planners. Clearly, this is an area of opportunity for leadership. The need is indisputable. Yet the library's neglect reflects that of our society in general. Each month the Bureau of Labor Statistics releases the nation's unemployment figures. In times of economic recession or high inflation, these figures are prominently displayed in newspaper headlines. Unemployment figures for youth are usually given little attention though they are often twice the rate of adult unemployment and for minority youths, several times higher!

Contrast this national attitude toward youth and library services with that of the USSR:

Until recently, Soviet teenagers were served at public libraries on the same basis as adults. The delegation was told that on the assumption that books perform a special service for young people, a system of libraries was created to fulfill the needs of the 14–20-year-old age group. Among the purposes of the youth libraries are: (1) to accustom teenagers to the use of libraries; (2) to "socialize and acculturate" youth; and (3) to provide a center for cultural education. In the Soviet Union, this age group comprises a population of forty million teenagers. There are at present 40,000 youth libraries or youth departments within public libraries. Since the initiation of this program, the number of teenage readers has increased.

This youth library is the republic center for methodological work. It is ten years old, with more than one million items in Russian and other languages.

With 40,000 readers, its annual circulation is about 1½ million items. The staff of 300 includes teachers, sociologists, psychologists and musicians. Seventeen research departments study the problem of the education of youth, publishing about 200 research works annually. In addition to being a methodological center for the Ministry of Education, the Library coordinates its work with several other relevant ministries.

Before the Library was organized, questionnaires were sent to 10,000 teenagers and sociologists to solicit opinions on the desired functions of the youth library. As well as lending to all teenagers, whether students or working, the Library is the center for discussion groups, clubs, music programs, and language courses.

The Library staff publish 29 indexes, both current and retrospective. Publication announcements are distributed. A recommended reading of about 400 books is the basis for advisory services to the users, based on an estimate of their free time and ability to read an average of 27–30 books annually. Phonograph records are produced as learning aids, including a record listing recommended readings. Among the indexes and bibliographies are an index of world literature, broken down by subject, a bibliography of youth abroad, and a bibliography on Soviet youth.

Much of the sociological and psychological research is aimed at occupational counseling and at "shaping patriotic feelings and attitudes toward other countries." [2]

This national approach to coordinating and planning library service for youth recognizes "that society's need of initiating, as it were, its younger members into a definite state of knowledge seems to reach back into man's biological past" [3, p. 37].

It has been the potential for reducing costs, not improving services, which has been the primary motivation behind the use of new technology in libraries. Nevertheless, the introduction of computer-based reference services has sharpened the skills of librarians and brought new services to users. While it is true that computers will be used increasingly in public libraries for administrative and technical service activities, it is perhaps the photocopying machine that is the form of new technology which has had the most pervasive effect on libraries. It alone has revolutionized study patterns and work habits for library staff and users alike, while making local, regional, and national resource sharing more of a reality through the national interlibrary lending system. Indeed, during the deliberations of the National Commission on New Technological Uses of Copyrighted Works, there was considerably less pressure to control computer uses of copyrighted works than there was to control uses of photocopying machines.

Another means of reducing costs while increasing the number of users served has been the movement toward larger units of service through public library systems and other cooperative ventures crossing jurisdictional boundaries. There is evidence that these systems have provided wider access to materials for their user communities, extended services to previously unserved populations, and increased the professional expertise of the librarians working in them. Though cost reduction for individual libraries has been a primary motivation for the development of public library systems, the systems have, at the same time, tended to increase library expenditures far beyond what might ordinarily be projected for member libraries operating independently.

But even these measures have not been enough to keep the wolf from the public library door. The decade of the 1970s is likely to be recorded in library history as notorious for reductions in library services. Reductions in hours of service, personnel layoffs, and drastically diminished revenues have been common among big city libraries. Nevertheless, in the midst of these problems some public libraries, principally in the southwestern United States, have prospered and perhaps even flourished. New central library buildings have gone up or are planned for Houston and Dallas. Cleveland and Columbus, Ohio, won substantial increases in revenues at the polls, while Indiana provided state aid to public libraries for the first time in history [4, p. 254].

The inconsistencies in public library financing are only the superficial manifestations of the confusion that exists over public support for libraries. Molz's identification of the principal weakness of the federal library programs, which have tended to be supported only by pressure from the professional library community, as being their isolation from broader educational programs could trigger a new strategy. Education continues to be a major objective of the public library, but librarians still have no clear perception of the public library's relationship to formal educational institutions or, indeed, of the many ways in which many persons continue their education informally. The new strategy requires a new concept of the public library and an identification of its most important allies and the most relevant services it can offer to them.

The Political Solution

"All other media of our society increase the power of the single speaker or writer, linking him or her to ever vaster audiences, reaching their peak in prime time network television, when a president may reach 50 million or more at one moment. Alone among the instruments of communications, the library throws its weight on the opposite side of the scale, increasing the power of the single inquirer by linking him or her with an ever vaster number of information sources" [5, p. 32]. This statement provides perhaps the most compelling rationale for the future services of public libraries in its modern communications setting. To fulfill the mission suggested by Lacy's statement is likely to depend heavily on two unfinished agenda items of American librarianship: politics and continuing professional education. As used here, this is politics with a small *p*. It refers to managing a complex of relationships with governmental bodies at the local, state, and federal level; with other education professionals; with publishing and the information industry; and with the multiple-interest communities within the public at large. Joeckel suggested in 1935 that the public library needed to move closer to public education as a means of fulfilling its basic educational mission [6]. Certainly, all of the service areas of librarianship have major competitors in the formal educational establishment. This is obviously true of library service to children where there is increasing competition from school libraries and media centers, but it also extends to services to young adults and to adult education. While these are traditional service areas for the public library, the shift to a formal educational system devoted to the total educational needs of the learner has left the public library without a generally accepted role in the educational process. This may be disputed in terms of the actual activities in which libraries are engaged, but it is certainly true in terms of national policies governing educational programs. There is some move for change, though it is likely to need far more stimulation than it has so far received.

We note, for example, a recent announcement from the U.S. Office of Education, reporting the availability of a report entitled "Individuals, Learning Opportunities, and Public Policy: A Life-Long Learning Perspective." This report was released in order to highlight an accrued emphasis of the Office of Education on life-long learning. It points out clearly that, while federal support has tended to emphasize activities taking place in postsecondary institutions rather than in less formal or less traditional settings, the new program it will sponsor will attempt to involve more of the less traditional institutions providing learning opportunities, including museums, public libraries, and educational television. While these are fine words, the facts of life within the Office of Education will certainly militate against any significant shift of the approximately $14 billion which presently go into learning opportunities for adults over the traditional college age. Perhaps what is needed is a political task force which can develop strategies for negotiating an appropriate series of opportunities for the public library in the educational process at all levels. This would include negotiating several patterns of relationships that might prevail in a given community for the provision of library services, whether in schools or for preschool age children. It might include establishing patterns for multitype cooperative activities among public, school, and academic libraries. It would possibly include negotiated agreements with secondary as well as post-secondary institutions for the provision of informal learning opportunities for students as well as out-of-school adults. Colman notes in this context that "a major organizational weakness of the American [public] library has been revealed in its frequent lack of success in involving

libraries of all types in many potentially promising new programs. . . . "
[7, p. 103]. He adds an appropriate note of caution: "These tasks are
delicate and controversial because they intrude upon the status quo" [7,
p. 103].

The Solution of Continuing Education

While this is a long-term matter for the unfinished agenda of American
librarianship, there is a more immediate agenda item which is more
directly within the control of the organized elements within the field.
American librarianship established the pattern of offering formal higher
education for librarianship with the publication of the Williamson report
in 1923. Nevertheless, only about half of the present-day working
librarians have formal education for their profession. Despite continuing efforts to upgrade and broaden library education, the formal library
educational establishment remains unable to influence to any significant
degree the vast majority of librarians in the field.

Moreover, for some years now librarians across the nation have
expressed concern that the knowledge and skills gained in pursuit of the
graduate library degree have not been sufficient to keep them abreast of
the rapid changes which have taken place within our society and within
the field of librarianship. These changes include technological developments as well as the increasing complexity of social, political, and
economic life in America. These expressions of concern are frequently
attached to the phrase "continuing professional education." As used
here, continuing professional education includes the means which
professional practitioners use in fulfilling their individual needs to
continue to learn and grow professionally. It consists of those learning
activities following preparatory education and work experience which
are designed primarily (1) to keep them abreast of new knowledge and
developments within their field, (2) to update their basic education, (3) to
refresh them in various aspects of their basic education, and (4) to
enhance their job competence. Such activities normally do not lead to
academic degrees or to formal advanced standing in the profession. Continuing education programs may be provided on a full-time or part-time
basis and may be formal or informal in organization, but they are usually
of relatively short duration. They are conducted in a great variety of
formats, using many methods and techniques, including transportable
learning laboratories and annual conferences of professional associations; and they are sponsored by a diverse group of institutions and
organizations.

A benchmark survey on the need for continuing professional education in librarianship was sponsored by the National Commission on

156   ROBERT WEDGEWORTH

Libraries and Information Science and appeared in May 1974. The report proposed a nationwide organization, which developed as the Continuing Library Education Network and Exchange (CLENE). This survey identified certain needs for continuing education which were either not being met or being met poorly and established five priority needs: updating, management training, human relations training, automation, and nonprint media [8].

CLENE has served admirably as a forum for library associations, library educators, and others to discuss the problems and needs of continuing education. It has also been a clearinghouse for disseminating information on the many continuing education opportunities that occur each year. Because it has been recognized that CLENE lacks a strong operational base with the necessary staff and facilities for further program expansion, there has been a growing interest in establishing a national center for continuing professional library education. The major purpose of the center would be to identify, create, package, and deliver continuing education programs to the library community at large.

An interesting aspect of the development of a national continuing education capability is the way in which such programs might be delivered into the field. In librarianship, we are familiar with workshops and institutes as well as extension courses; we are less familiar with home-study courses. In addition to these traditional delivery methods, it is quite conceivable that courses could be offered via telecommunications for certain topics of national interest. This could mean regional or national telephonic hookups of audiences at multiple locations to a single source offering programs. Or it could mean the transmission of a program from a single source via a satellite connection to multiple receiving points. It was partly to test this latter capability that the American Library Association recently experimented with the use of satellite telecommunications in order to bring a program on copyright, a subject of broad national interest, to a group of librarians in thirteen southern states. Our experience with satellite telecommunications as a delivery mechanism for a continuing education program was encouraging, and this certainly should be considered a specific component of any proposed national program.

Some basic assumptions which might guide the development of a national continuing education program are:

1. The program should include at least a general component, for example, the creation and delivery of a broad variety of continuing education subject packages of general interest. It should also include a special component, the major purpose of which would be to assist specialized organizations in the creation and delivery of continuing education programs of special interest to their members or staff.

2. The program should concentrate upon those practitioners who

already possess the first professional degree or who are operating at a professional level.

3. The program should make use of existing library schools and their faculties as a major resource for the system and should assume a complimentarity with library school programs to avoid significant overlap and duplication.

4. The program may or may not include a system for recognizing participation.

5. The program should utilize a high level of media technology in the creation and packaging of course materials.

6. After an initial research and demonstration phase, the program should support itself from fees and the sale of support materials.

7. The program should focus initially upon developing courses to address the problems and needs of public librarians but should move immediately thereafter to address other areas.

What, then, would be the appropriate audience for this program of continuing education? There are at least three target audiences. First, the library specialist, defined as working librarians below the management level who apply their skills to the various services offered within the library. It can be assumed that the technical processing skills of library specialists need upgrading and that they have a need for improved how-to-do-it courses, which also take into account implications for future developments. Second, middle management, defined as working librarians who oversee a given procedure or specialty, and whose skills are applied to the integration of personnel and processes within a defined area. It can be assumed that middle managers need to develop their perceptive and evaluative skills relative to personnel and procedures alike, and that these include diagnostic and remedial problem solving. Third, senior management, defined as librarians operating at top policy and fiscal levels, responsible for administering a library system and integrating it within the larger structure of which it is a component. It can be assumed that they need to become sufficiently versed in systems and communication theory to allow the realistic evaluation of developments and trends. They would benefit from in-depth political analyses that would assist them in their dealings with various governmental and other jurisdictional bodies which effect the growth of library programs. They may also need a grounding in fundamental areas of management, which ought to include, for example, financial courses for nonfinancial executives. It is possible that some courses could overlap the different target audiences. However, identifying these would at least establish the basic levels at which the various continuing education programs could operate.

The subject matter of the continuing education program broadly construed is likely to fall into three basic areas of librarianship: the management of libraries and information systems, services to various categories of users, and the processes and procedures of technical services. There are likely to be additional offerings in areas such as communications and human relations.

No program of this type has a reasonable chance of success without the cooperation and support of the graduate library schools, which provide basic professional education in the field. The continuing education program being discussed here would attempt to utilize the expertise represented by the faculties of these institutions, insofar as their schedules permitted. Beyond the field of library education, consultants might be needed to create courses in many different areas.

If we build on the expertise and confidence that exist within the field of librarianship, as well as on the resources and facilities of graduate library schools, it is possible that a superior continuing education system could be established which would have a standard curriculum and testing program. Though centrally administered, monitored, and revised in consultation with elements of the organized library profession, that program could embody a wide range of choices. A few of the benefits which might accrue from such a program would be the provision of a continuing education curriculum which could be used nationally. It could provide assistance to graduate library schools by providing an enrichment mechanism for staff and alumni as well as for the community of local users. It could establish an appropriate national institutional structure in which professional educators and library practitioners could engage in a dialogue which could help in the development of adequate educational responses to practical needs. It could encourage better communication within the profession by bringing together practitioners of diverse backgrounds and experiences to study together. It could stimulate additional research as more practitioners enhance their knowledge and skills. It could initiate an important area of cooperation with professional colleagues in the international marketplace as common problems are attacked. Some examples of these problems are certain information-handling techniques, library building programs for certain climatic conditions, and the provision of library services to certain narrowly defined categories of users.

As previously indicated, the adoption of a recognition system needs further study. However, the program being discussed here will need not only a research and evaluation system to assess its performance but perhaps also a career-counseling program using diagnostic as well as self-assessment tools as input to the research and evaluation phase. This entire program should operate at a very high level of quality and be self-supporting. This means that the courses may be considerably more expensive than the present pattern for library workshops and institutes. However, recognizable quality always justifies additional expense.

Any continuing education system must meet two requirements. It must give effective education to students, and the program results must be translatable into improved status for practitioners. Putting into perspective the areas which have been covered by the papers given in this seminar—the media, services to users, technology, the administration and development of larger units of service—it is obvious that personnel will be the key to the public library taking advantage of all of the opportunities that are represented by these areas, as well as dealing with their associated problems. The politics of librarianship is not something that is intuitive. It is something to which the organized profession must make a major commitment in order to develop political skills within its ranks.

These two action-oriented strategies for assisting the public library could create the possibility of this institution being able more than just to survive into the twenty-first century. They also subscribe to the "can do" philosophy exemplified by our earliest generation of library leaders, while recognizing the limitations within which the public library as well as the public librarian will continue to serve.

REFERENCES

1. Gaines, Ervin. "The Large Municipal Library as a Network." *Library Quarterly* 39 (January 1969): 41–51.
2. Delougaz, Nathalie; Martin, Susan K.; and Wedgeworth, Robert. *Libraries and Information Services in the U.S.S.R.* Unpublished report of a U.S. State Department–sponsored exchange visit to the Soviet Union, November 16–26, 1976. Available from the International Relations Officer, American Library Association, Chicago.
3. Butler, Pierce. *An Introduction to Library Science*. Chicago: University of Chicago Press, 1961.
4. Wallis, C. Lamar. "Public Libraries." In *The ALA Yearbook*, edited by Robert Wedgeworth. Chicago: American Library Association, 1977.
5. Lacy, Dan. "Libraries and the Freedom of Access to Information." In *Libraries and the Life of the Mind in America*. Chicago: American Library Association, 1977.
6. Joeckel, Carleton B. *Government of the Public Library*. Chicago: University of Chicago Press, 1935.
7. Colman, William G. "Federal and State Financial Interest in the Performance and Promise of Library Networks." *Library Quarterly* 39 (January 1969): 99–108.
8. *Continuing Library and Information Science Education: Final Report to the National Commission on Libraries and Information Science*. Washington, D.C.: Government Printing Office, 1974.

THE CONTRIBUTORS

MAE BENNE: professor, School of Librarianship, University of Washington. Born Morrowville, Kansas, 1924. B.S., University of Nebraska, 1950; M.S.L.S., University of Illinois, 1955. Publications include: "Leavening for the Youth Culture," *Wilson Library Bulletin* 52 (December 1977): 312–18; *Policies and Practices Affecting Juvenile Library Collections in County and Regional Libraries in Washington State* (Seattle: School of Librarianship, University of Washington, 1970); and *Central Children's Library in Metropolitan Public Libraries* (Seattle: School of Librarianship, University of Washington, 1977).

GENEVIEVE M. CASEY: professor, Division of Library Science, Wayne State University. Born Minneapolis, 1916. B.S., College of St. Catherine, 1937; M.L.S., University of Michigan, 1956. Publications include: "Library Service to the Handicapped and Institutionalized," *Library Trends* 20 (October 1971): 350–66; *Public Library Service to the Illiterate Adult*, ED 067 133 (Detroit: Wayne State University, 1972); *Public Library Service to the Urban Disadvantaged* (Detroit: Wayne State University, 1972); "Staffing Library Service to the Aging," *Library Trends* 21 (January 1973): 413–30; "Library and Information Needs of Aging Americans," in *Library and Information Needs of the Nation: Proceedings of a Conference on the Needs of Occupational, Ethnic and Other Groups in the United States* (Washington, D.C.: National Commission on Libraries and Information Science, 1974); *The Public Library in the Network Mode: A Preliminary Investigation*, ED 098 900 (Washington, D.C.: U.S. Office of Education, 1974); "Services to the Disadvantaged," *Library Trends* 23 (October 1974): 271–85; and "Federal Aid to Libraries," *Library Trends*, vol. 24 (ed.) (July 1975).

MARY K. CHELTON: assistant professor, Graduate School of Library Service, Rutgers University. Born Baltimore, 1942. B.A., Mount Saint Agnes College, 1963; M.L.S., Rutgers University, 1965. Publications include: "Booktalking: You Can Do It!" *School Library Journal* 22 (April 1976): 39–43; "Surrogate Mothers vs. Surrogate Teenagers," *Booklegger* 3 (Spring 1976): 39–41; "Adolescent Sexuality: A Self-training Bibliography," *Emergency Librarian* (November–December 1977): 6–9; and "Young Adult Services: You Can Do It!" *North Carolina Libraries* 35 (Winter 1978): 23–32.

THOMAS CHILDERS: associate professor, Graduate School of Library Science, Drexel University. Born Chillicothe, Ohio, 1940. B.A., University of Maryland, 1962; M.L.S., 1963, and Ph.D., 1970, Rutgers University. Publications include: *Information Service in Public Libraries: Two Studies* (with Terence Crowley) (Metuchen, N.J.: Scarecrow Press, 1971); "Municipal Funding of Library Services" (with Beth Krevitt), *American Libraries* 3 (January 1972): 53–57; "Managing the Quality of Library Reference/Information Service," *Library Quarterly* 42 (April 1972): 212–17; "Statistics That Describe Libraries and Library Service," in *Advances in Librarianship* (New York: Academic Press, 1975), vol. 5; *The Information-Poor in America* (Metuchen, N.J.: Scarecrow Press, 1975); and "The Neighborhood Information Center Project," *Library Quarterly* 46 (July 1976): 271–89.

KENNETH E. DOWLIN: director, Pikes Peak Regional Library District, Colorado Springs, Colorado. Born Wray, Colorado, 1941. B.A., University of Colorado, 1963; M.A.L.S., University of Denver, 1966. Publications include: "Libraries in Isolation: A Plan of Attack," *Library Journal* 93 (March 15, 1968): 116; "CATV + NCPL = VRS," *Library Journal* 95 (September 1, 1970): 2768–70; "Can a Library Find Happiness in the Big Cruel World of Television?" *Wilson Library Bulletin* 47 (May 1973): 763–67; and "Community Information Center: Talk or Action?" (with Elizabeth Fuller), in *The Use of Computers and Related Reference Activities in Libraries*, edited by F. Wilfrid Lancaster (Champaign: Graduate School of Library Science, University of Illinois, 1976).

MARY JO LYNCH: program officer, American Library Association. Born Detroit, 1939. B.A., Marygrove College, 1961: A.M.L.S., University of Michigan, 1962; M.A., University of Detroit, 1966; Ph.D., Rutgers University, 1977. Publications include: "A New Approach to the Guided Tour," *RQ* 11 (Fall 1971): 46–48; "RSD and ASD: Getting It All Together," *American Libraries* 2 (May 1971): 501–3; "Women in Reference Service," in *Women in the Library Profession: Leadership Roles and Contributions* (Ann Arbor: University of Michigan School of Library Science, 1971); "Academic Library Reference Policy Statements," *RQ* 11 (Spring 1972): 222–26; "Bibliographic Instruction in Academic Libraries: New Developments" (with Thomas Kirk), *Drexel Library Quarterly* 8 (July 1972): 357–65; "Trials, Tactics, and Timing: Some Thoughts on Library Instruction Programs," in *A Challenge for Academic Libraries*, edited by Sul H. Lee (Ann Arbor, Mich.: Pierian Press, 1973): "Library Tours: The First Step," in *Educating the Library User*, edited by John Lubans (New York: R. R. Bowker Co., 1974); "Work Experience and Observation in a General Reference Course—More on 'Theory vs. Practice' " (with George Whitbeck), *Journal of Education for Librarianship* 15 (Spring 1975): 271–80; "Design for Diversity: Alternatives to Standards for Public Libraries" (with Ralph Blasingame), *PLA Newsletter* 13 (June 1974): 4–22, also published in *Studies in Library Management*, vol. 3, edited by Gileon Holroyd (Hamden, Conn.: Linnet Books; London: Clive Bingley, 1976); *New Jersey Measurement Study: A Study to Refine and Test New Measures of Library Service and Train Library Personnel in Their Use*, with Philip M. Clark, Ellen C. Clark, and Ernest R. DeProspo (New Brunswick, N.J.: Rutgers University Graduate School of Library Service, Bureau of Library and Information Science Research, 1976); and "Reference Interviews in Public Libraries," *Library Quarterly* 48 (April 1978): 119–42.

R. KATHLEEN MOLZ: professor, School of Library Service, Columbia University. Born Baltimore, 1928. B.S., 1949, and M.A., 1950, Johns Hopkins University; M.A., University of Michigan, 1953; D.L.S., Columbia University, 1976. Publications include: "The Public Library: The People's University?" *American Scholar* 34 (Winter 1964–65): 95–102; "The Public Custody of the High Pornography," *American Scholar* 36 (Winter 1966–67): 93–101; *The Metropolitan Library* (ed., with Ralph W. Conant) (Cambridge, Mass.: M.I.T. Press, 1972); *Federal Policy and Library Support* (Cambridge, Mass.: M.I.T. Press, 1976); and "Libraries and the Development and Future of Tax Support," in *Libraries and the Life of the Mind in America* (Chicago: American Library Association, 1977).

LORNA VINCENT PAULIN: formerly county librarian, Hertfordshire County Library, England. Born Bexley, Kent, England, 1914. B.A., 1934, and M.A., 1936, University College, London. Publications include various articles in professional journals.

W. Boyd Rayward: associate professor, Graduate Library School, University of Chicago, and editor, *Library Quarterly*. Born Inverell, New South Wales, Australia, 1939. B.A., University of Sydney, 1959; Dip. Lib., University of New South Wales, 1964; M.S., University of Illinois at Urbana-Champaign, 1965; Ph.D., University of Chicago, 1973. Publications include: "Systematic Bibliography in England, 1850–1895," *Occasional Paper No. 84* (Urbana-Champaign: Graduate School of Library Science, University of Illinois, 1967); "The UDC and FID: A Historical Perspective," *Library Quarterly* 37 (July 1967): 259–78; "Libraries as Organizations," *College and Research Libraries* 30 (July 1969): 312–26; *The Universe of Information: The Work of Paul Otlet for Documentation and International Organisation*, FID Publication no. 520 (Moscow: VINITI, 1975); "Librarianship in the New World and the Old: Some Points of Contact," *Library Trends* 25 (July 1976): 209–26; *The Variety of Librarianship: Essays in Honour of John Wallace Metcalfe* (ed.) (Sydney: Library Association of Australia, 1976); "Subject Access to the Catalogue of Scientific Papers, 1800–1900," in *The Variety of Librarianship* (see above); "Some Developments in Nineteenth Century Bibliography: England," *Libri* 27 (June 1977): 97–107; and "The Local Node in Multi-Type Library Networks," in *Multi-Type Library Cooperation*, edited by Beth Hamilton and William B. Ernst (New York: R. R. Bowker Co., 1977).

Gordon Stevenson: associate professor, School of Library and Information Science, State University of New York at Albany. Born Washington, Pennsylvania, 1924. B.M., 1948, and M.A., 1950, Duquesne University; M.A., 1956, and Ph.D., 1970, Indiana University. Publications include: "The Mainzer Sachkatalog and Its Background," *Library Quarterly* 40 (July 1970): 318–39; "Discography: Scientific, Analytical, Historical and Systematic," *Library Trends* 21 (July 1972): 101–35; "Sound Recordings," in *Advances in Librarianship* (New York: Academic Press, 1975), vol. 5; "Popular Culture and the Public Library," in *Advances in Librarianship* (New York: Academic Press, 1977), vol. 7; and "The Wayward Scholar: Resources and Research in Popular Culture," *Library Trends* 25 (April 1977): 779–818.

Robert Wedgeworth: executive director, American Library Association. Born Ennis, Texas, 1937. A.B., Wabash College, 1959; M.L.S., University of Illinois at Urbana-Champaign, 1961. Publications include: "Brown University Library Fund Accounting System," *Journal of Library Automation* 1 (March 1968): 51–65; "Foreign Blanket Orders: Precedent and Practice," *Library Resources and Technical Services* 14 (Spring 1970); 258–68; *ALA Yearbook* (ed.) (Chicago: American Library Association, 1976–); "Organizing Librarians: Three Options for ALA," *Library Journal* 101 (January 1976): 213–15; "Global Library Diplomacy: Building National Purpose for an International Mission," *American Libraries* 9 (January 1978): 33–34; *ALA Encyclopedia* (ed.) (Chicago: American Library Association, in press); "Libraries," *World Book Encyclopedia*, 1978 edition (in press).